Praise for Betty: A Memoir

A fully absorbing and inherently engaging read, 'Betty: A Memoir' is an extraordinary life story that is a riveting read from first page to last. Exceptionally well written, organized and presented, 'Betty: A Memoir' is a compelling and unreservedly recommended addition to community, college, and university library Contemporary American Biography collections. By turns heart-breaking, empathy invoking, and ultimately inspiring...
~ *Midwest Book Review*

...With **a novelist's eye for detail,** Mary McSwain Steele evokes the sense of place of southwestern Wisconsin as few writers ever have, her description rivaling David Rhodes' bestselling novel, *Driftless.* The author threads her narrative through not just memories of her mother, but the journey Steele embarked upon to learn more about her father and his first family, including a half-brother she never met. Especially poignant is how, after not seeing her father since she was too young to remember his face, she finally found his forgotten grave in a Florida cemetery. Steele's story of how she and her sister, Susan, helped their mother fight her losing battle with cancer is a gripping testament of how two loving, caring daughters returned the love of their mother.
~ **Des Moines Register**

This book is **a gorgeously written narrative of grief, love, imperfection, grace**, and redemption through family relationships. I could not put it down, even with all my kids running around my house during snow days. I am someone who usually takes months to read a book because of work and children keeping me so busy I can't find the time. But the time found me with this book. I loved it and finished it in two days. As a single mother, I found so much of my life echoed in Betty's... and found great hope and peace in the narrative of deep love, acceptance, and devotion in Betty's children and family. It was healing to read and I know I will find myself recommending this to others and going back to it myself in the future. ~ *Sarah, LA*

This **well-written book is so engaging that it stays with you for days** after you've finished reading it. The author centers her story on the final days of her mother's life, as she loses her battle with cancer. During this time of caring for her mother, the author reflects on her childhood years spent in a small midwestern community in the 1950s and 60s. Poignant memories of her siblings, grandparents, friends, school and community are probably not unlike those of others who grew up in the era. However, the honest assessment she shares of her complex relationship with her mother and the challenges of growing up in a single parent household sets her story apart from many. Her cathartic journey allows her to come to terms with the difficult mother-daughter dynamic, an absent alcoholic father, and the painful loss of a sibling. A surprising deathbed confession leaves the author with a new challenge to face, and leaves the reader wanting more. Warning: Once you start reading, you will not want to put this book down! ~ *Julie, WI*

Betty is **a powerful memoir of a woman who lived and died with courage and grace.** Eloquently written by her daughter, Mary McSwain Steele, this book is a transforming experience and a beautiful testament to a remarkable woman. Mary expertly blends emails, hospice notes, photos, cards, sentiments, and reminiscences into a touching and memorable book. I couldn't put this book down! ~ *Mary, KS*

I recently finished reading Betty: A Memoir. The author, Mary McSwain Steele, has done an **excellent job on every level**, from capturing small town life in a different era, to sharing the gift and grief of caring for her terminally ill mother. The author expertly combines both stories lovingly, without glossing over the challenges of her divorced mother raising three children, or the pain of the death of her mother. This is a book with heart, courageously told without being overly sentimental. It made me smile and it made me cry. All in all, the book is a well written story of love, loss and life. ~ *Rene, FL*

Mary McSwain Steele's **beautifully written and truly moving memoir** is a must read for anyone who is a parent, or who had one. "Betty" got me thinking a lot about my mom, things I wished

I had asked her, her final days, etc. when I know I was the last family member to speak with her, and would I have had the strength of character (and patience) to be the loving caregiver and Mary and her sister Susan were. Thank you so much for sharing your mom and her story of courage, grit, love, heartbreak, and adventure with the rest of us. ~ *Lori, IA*

I had another book in front of this one but decided to just take a peek... and, well, **it sucked me in.** I'm feeling so many things after finishing it but at the top is just deep gratitude. I'm grateful for this reminder about the importance of connection, of family, of asking questions and deeply listening - before it's too late. I learned so much about the author, her mother, her family and yet there were so many universal themes. One: We all have 'stuff' no matter how it looks from the outside. The author did an incredible job of structuring this story. It will stay with me for a long time. ~ *Annie, NC*

The author takes the readers on **her journey of acceptance and recovery** from the death of her mother, Betty. She walks you through her experiences growing up in a small midwestern town and the struggles Betty encountered as a single parent. She shares the transformation of her relationship with Betty and her emotional turmoil in overcoming her grief. You will see yourself or someone you know as the author grapples with the end-of-life emotions she describes as she cares for Betty. This book is well worth reading. ~ *Sheila, WI*

This book has something for everyone. The author shares her mother's last days... "Betty" will leave you admiring her mother and identifying with this family's struggles and victories. ~ *Mar*

My next pick for Book Club! Betty is both heartwarming and heartbreaking, and I couldn't put it down. Loved the beautifully written description of growing up in a rural community in the 1950s and 1960s. And I teared up at the author's graceful depiction of the complicated but deep love between a mother and a daughter. Just a great read for anyone who has ever had a mother. ~ *Jane, IA*

Betty

A Single Mother's Courage
in Life and Death and Her Daughter's
Struggle to Cope with Grief

Mary McSwain Steele

Dedication

I am so blessed to have Susan McSwain Garvin as my sister. She is, and always has been, a natural caregiver. Susan's love and compassion for our mother, as well as her dedication, stamina, and desire to be with Mom 24 hours a day for 32 days, helped make those last days so special and meaningful for all of us. Together, we were able to provide a level of care that I could have never accomplished alone. I can only hope that if I ever need end-of-life care, she will be around for me.

Contents

If ever there is a tomorrow
when we're not together,
there is something
you must always remember.
You are braver than you believe,
stronger than you seem,
and smarter than you think.
But the most important thing is,
even if we're apart,
I'll always be with you.

-Winnie the Pooh

1
Thirty-Two Days

Day 1: Dec. 12, 2008

When the doctor walked into my mom's hospital room, I had a sick feeling he wasn't bringing good news. He didn't trivialize the message that he came to deliver by beginning with small talk. Instead, he got right to the point, telling Mom the endometrial cancer for which she'd had surgery a few months earlier was back and had spread throughout her abdomen. There was nothing they could do for her.

Mom turned to my sister and me with a look of stunned disbelief and said, "Well, that's a bummer." Not the response you would expect from an 84-year-old woman after hearing a terminal diagnosis, but certainly not an inaccurate one.

My sister, Susan, and I sat on the small leather sofa, unable to move, trying to absorb what the doctor was telling us. The prognosis was about as bad as it gets. We asked what Mom's options were. He told us about another of his patients with the same diagnosis who was much younger than Mom. That patient had opted for treatment, he said, "but it didn't turn out well."

Because the malignant mass throughout her abdomen had caused a bowel blockage, Mom would not be able to eat or drink without severe nausea. She would probably die of dehydration within a few weeks. The tumor would continue to grow, and she would need strong pain medication. After a painfully awkward silence, Susan and I finally had the presence of mind to get up off the sofa and go to Mom's bedside, hold her hand, stroke her hair, and try to offer some measure of comfort. Her doctor asked if we had questions. We did, but where do you begin?

Hearing the prognosis, my mom looked at her doctor and then at us, with tears slowly running down her cheeks, and stoically said, "Just keep me comfortable." The doctor nodded and quietly left the room.

My mom, Elizabeth McSwain, known to everyone as Betty, was a retired nurse. She raised my brother, my sister, and me by herself, and then traveled the world for 10 years. She'd had her share of challenges in life, including two previous bouts of cancer, but this diagnosis would prove to be her toughest, and it would be her final one. Her life was affected by trauma, but not defined by it. She lived on her terms, and she would die on her terms.

And so began an important chapter in our lives – my mother's, my sister's, and mine. We didn't know it at the time, but our mom had only 32 days left on this earth. A month and a day. I knew it would be awful seeing Mom get weaker, potentially in severe pain, and then watching her die, but I didn't expect that time to be beautiful as well. During her final days, Susan and I learned more about the imperfect yet remarkable woman who raised us. We reminisced, laughed, and cried. We wrote her obituary together and learned more about our family history, including long-kept secrets that stunned my sister and me.

As the solemn doctor gently laid out my mom's diagnosis that began her final fight, I could not have expected how this moment would change me. Grieving my mother's illness and then her death, I felt a strong desire to learn more about the man she married, our father, who was only in my life for a few years. I found not only a hidden treasure of new and fascinating information, but I also developed meaningful relationships with people I'd never met, and I met family members I never knew existed.

2

Elizabeth Anna Rosson McSwain

I don't know much about my mom's growing-up years, but after she died, I found a few pages of penciled notes among her papers with the title "Memoir." Beneath the title, she'd written some thoughts about her childhood. She described herself as having "red hair and buck teeth," and she was "tall, skinny, and shy."

Mom wrote that she was on a federal program because she was so thin as a child. "I got to eat chocolate and tomato soup because I was so skinny." According to my mom's sparse memoir notes, she was the youngest child in her first-grade class, only 5½. By the time she was in her late teens, she was a tall, slender, attractive young woman as evidenced by the few photos I have of her early years.

Mom graduated in 1941 from Readstown High School in southwest Wisconsin. She entered nurse's training in September 1942 at Saint Francis School of Nursing, Viterbo College, in La Crosse, Wisconsin. Upon becoming a registered nurse in 1945, she worked at the highly regarded Gunderson Clinic in La Crosse before enlisting in the U.S. Army Nurse Corps in 1947. She always wanted to travel and

Mom graduated from Readstown High School at age 17 in 1941.

joining the Army was a way for her to earn a salary while seeing the country.

While looking through her educational documents, I noticed there was a one-year gap between Mom's high school graduation and her entrance into nurses' training at St. Francis. I'm sure she hadn't forgotten those details because her mind was sharp even at 84. Maybe she didn't think it was important. It seemed like a small detail at the time, so I put it aside in my mind.

Most days when I was growing up, Mom wore her white nurses' uniform – a shirtwaist dress that buttoned up the front, and her starched nursing cap. I was about six when

I first realized my mom was pretty. She had just come from my great-uncle's funeral, and she was wearing a black dress, pearl necklace, and pearl earrings – all things I'd never seen her wear before. I don't remember seeing her dressed up until that day. I told Mom she looked nice in the black dress. She seemed surprised but pleased. It wasn't a compliment she heard often.

Mom received a degree from St. Francis School of Nursing, Viterbo College, in La Crosse in 1945.

Throughout her life, Mom was happiest when she was outside. She loved flowers and enjoyed digging in her vegetable garden. She would often hike up the hill behind our house hunting for berries, morel mushrooms, wild asparagus, rhubarb, and hickory nuts. Mom was very careful about poisonous plants, but one time she came in contact with poison oak and had a severe reaction. She was hospitalized for several days with numbness on one side of her face. Although most of the numbness went away eventually, there was some permanent nerve damage causing the left side of her mouth to droop. Mom was self-conscious about how it affected her appearance and her inability to drink out of a bottle without a straw.

One of my favorite photos of Mom, with a deer friend.
I don't know when, where, or why the picture was taken.

My mom loved animals, especially dogs and birds. As a child, her family had an Airedale Terrier named Duke, a cat, and chickens, according to her memoir notes. When my sister, my brother, and I were in elementary school, a stray German Shepherd started hanging around our house. Mom said we could keep her, and we were delighted. We named the dog Duchess. Mom thought Duchess had been mistreated

7

because she would cower and whine whenever she heard thunder, gunshots, or firecrackers. Duchess was an outdoor dog, but Mom let her in the house during storms, hunting seasons, and on the Fourth of July.

There was a day after my siblings and I went off to college when my mom thought Duchess was sick and probably close to death. Mom said she got out the shovel and dug a hole in the backyard in which to bury our dog. She talked to Duchess, with tears running down her cheeks, as she shoveled dirt. "I cried and dug, cried and dug," she told us a little sheepishly. As Mom was digging the grave, Duchess started perking up, and soon our dog was back to normal. Mom joyfully shoveled the dirt back into the hole. Duchess kept her company for many more of her empty-nest years.

My mom was given this basset hound which was the runt of a litter. She named him George and spoon fed him from birth. My brother, Mike, gave her the sweatshirt with George's picture on it.

3
Third Time's the Charm?

The terminal diagnosis of endometrial cancer was not my mom's only experience with serious illness. The first of three bouts of cancer was in 1993. The diagnosis was rectal cancer. She gave careful consideration to her options. Mom often had said she wouldn't subject herself to extreme treatments, regardless of the diagnosis or prognosis. She had seen patients who received radical treatment for rectal cancer during her nursing career and remembering what they had to endure still haunted her. When she was several years younger, she was having heart palpitations. Mom said if the doctor told her she needed a pacemaker, not generally considered an extreme treatment, she would refuse. We were relieved when the cardiologist told her to consume less caffeine and avoid stress, and no other procedure was necessary.

Knowing how she felt about extreme treatments, we were surprised when Mom agreed to radiation, a procedure with potentially negative side effects. We drove her to Sioux City, Iowa, almost 100 miles from our home in Spencer, for out-patient treatments. It was January, and on one occasion, we came home in a blizzard. Just when we thought we'd have to pull off the road and wait it out, creating a hazard for us as well as any traffic behind us, the wind died down, the skies cleared, and we were able to make it home safely. Mom told me I'd done a good job of driving. It is telling how vividly I remember that trip and her praise.

Mom aced her checkups over the next few years and was happy to pass the five-year mark and then the ten-year mark of being cancer-free. But in May 2008, she began to have some abdominal pain and vaginal bleeding. She must have known these symptoms could indicate a serious condition, but she put off getting checked. When she finally went to see her doctor, he did a PAP test which came out positive for cancer. He immediately referred her to a gynecologist who told her she had a tumor in the lining of her uterus and recommended a hysterectomy.

Resistant as always to any kind of medical procedure, she asked him, "What if I choose not to have the surgery?"

He replied, "You don't want to do that. Endometrial cancer is not a good way to die."

A biopsy showed it was a malignant mixed Mullerian tumor (MMMT). While researching MMMTs, I read that one cause could be radiation. The radiation she'd received for rectal cancer may have triggered the malignant tumor. When we told Mom that theory, she felt betrayed. I was surprised by her reaction. Maybe she thought if she hadn't agreed to radiation for rectal cancer, she wouldn't have gotten the endometrial tumor. But it's more likely she wouldn't have survived long enough to get endometrial cancer.

Mom decided to have the hysterectomy, I think in part because she liked the gynecologist. In chatting with him, she learned that he had been in the Army and stationed at Ft. Sam Houston in San Antonio where she had also been stationed for training. The surgery was delayed because Mom wanted to attend a family wedding and her all-school reunion later in the summer. After those events, my sister and I had schedule conflicts, and the gynecologist went on vacation.

Mom finally had the surgery in July 2008. It went well. The gynecologist told her, "We think we got it all. The tumor was encapsulated and—not to sound crass—but it was like shelling peanuts. It popped right out."

He told Mom she could see an oncologist if she wanted, but he was satisfied the cancer was gone. Mom was fine with that. She trusted him and had no desire to see another specialist. Maybe she was afraid an oncologist would have a different opinion. I think now how easy it would have been to make one more appointment, get one more opinion. I'll never know if it would have made any difference.

Two months after the surgery, my husband, Steve, and I took Mom to the ER with severe pain. She had a bowel blockage, probably caused by scar tissue from the hysterectomy. The doctor suggested waiting to see if the bowel would unkink itself. If not, it would require surgery, but the ER doctor said it wasn't unusual to have this kind of complication after an operation. Mom had just started golfing again after recovering from the hysterectomy. She asked the doctor if that might have contributed to the kinked bowel. An avid golfer, he told Mom he would never blame anything bad on golf, making her laugh. They chatted about their golf games while she waited to be admitted.

As it turned out, the surgery was needed, and Mom returned home a week later. She never complained about pain, but I noticed she was moving gingerly several weeks later. I wondered at the time if that was normal.

On the evening of December 11, Mom called me, sounding weak and scared. We took her to the ER again. She had the same symptoms as before: nausea, vomiting, pain in her abdomen. We were certain it was another bowel blockage like the last time, but the ER doctor ordered an X-ray. I cornered him in the hallway, out of Mom's earshot, and asked, "Why an X-ray? Why not proceed as before – wait to see if the bowel unkinks and if not, then proceed with surgery?"

He hesitated for what seemed like a long time and then said, "I think there is some kind of mass throughout her abdomen."

I didn't know exactly what that meant, but I knew it wasn't just another bowel blockage. We didn't tell Mom right away. She had survived rectal cancer, surgery for endometrial cancer, and now this. We hoped for the best – that she would agree to treatment and recover like before. Mom may have had a premonition that this time there might be a different outcome.

"I wonder which applies," she mused. "Third time's a charm? Or three strikes and you're out?" We would learn twenty-four hours later when her doctor told her the bad news: she had a malignant mass for which there was no cure or treatment.

Strike three.

4
Grandma and Grandad Rosson

His name was Albert. Her name was Ellyn. They were my mom's parents, my grandparents.

"Ellyn" wasn't the name her mom and dad, Walter and Anna York, gave her when she was born on October 6, 1898. Not exactly, anyway. Her given name was Ellen, spelled the traditional way. When Grandma was sixteen, she and her friend, Helen, decided to change the spelling of their names. They replaced the second "e" with a "y". Not only was the new spelling unique and slightly rebellious, it was also a symbolic link between two girls who would remain best friends for life. They never made it a legal name change, but they were known as Ellyn and Helyn from that point on.

At age 17, Ellyn May York married Albert Ernest Rosson, who was 19. They had three children. Alice was born in 1916, Raymond in 1917, and finally, seven years later, my mom, Elizabeth Anna, in 1924. Mom was born in the neighbor's home next door. The five of them, along with Albert's father and brother, lived in a small three-bedroom house in Readstown, a little village in southwest Wisconsin. Grandma and Grandad bought the house for $650 and made monthly payments on it. There was a cookstove in the kitchen and a wood stove in the living room. Grandad hunted for squirrels to supplement their meals, and Grandma made bread almost every day. The milkman delivered a glass bottle of milk to their doorstep daily.

Standing: My grandad and grandma, Albert & Ellyn Rosson
Seated: Ellyn's parents (my great-grandparents),
Robert (holding my cousin Gene) & Anna York

After I was grown and married, I asked Grandma Rosson why she married so young. She blushed, giggled self-consciously, and shocked me when she replied, "Because I had to." She went on to say, "Mary, we didn't know anything about where babies came from back then." I laughed at her confession. Some things don't change much from generation to generation except that most teens today know where babies come from.

Grandma Rosson had a pleasant personality but was more temperamental than Grandad. She was anxious and had a nervous habit of biting her fingernails. It was easy to make her laugh, which my sister and I did frequently as teenagers. Grandma went to the beauty parlor to have her hair tinted, but Susan and I often set it in pin curls for her. After washing her hair in the kitchen sink, we sectioned it off and curled her short locks around our index fingers, securing the curls in place with bobby pins. When the curls were dry, we combed them out. Grandma was always appreciative of our efforts and happy with the results. She was also glad to have saved money, maybe $2 or $3, by not having it done at the beauty parlor.

Grandad worked for the railroad and then as an inspector at the tobacco warehouse in Readstown. Grandma was a tobacco inspector, too, until she had children. Later in life, she was a correspondent for the *La Crosse Tribune*, the *Vernon County Broadcaster-Censor*, and the *Kickapoo Scout* simultaneously. She also wrote for the local weekly paper, *The Readstown Special*, starting in 1965. Grandma typed Readstown's local news using sheets of carbon paper so she could send each newspaper a copy without having to type the original several times.

Every Monday morning, Grandma phoned her friends and neighbors to ask if they had any news to report. Nearly everyone she called was happy to share information from the previous week about visitors, reunions, family dinners, or new babies – "chicken dinner stories." (In explaining chicken dinner stories to my grandson, Sam, he replied, "Oh, kind of like Facebook!") Grandma got paid by the line, so the more news she reported, the bigger her paycheck.

Grandma collected all the editions of *The Readstown Special* and kept them in a box under her bed. She knew I was interested in writing, and, many years later, I would receive a degree in journalism. Grandma told me I could have her copies of *The Readstown Special* when she was "done with them" – her euphemism for when she died.

Grandad was a quiet, gentle man. I thought he was

handsome, with a full head of silvery hair and darkly tanned skin. He and Grandma would sit outside in brightly painted metal lawn chairs with clamshell-shaped backs. There was always work to be done even while sitting in the backyard.

Grandma and Grandad would spread newspapers across their laps and together they would sort berries, snap beans, or pick the meat out of walnut shells, depending on the season.

Grandad called all of his grandchildren "Bub." I'm not sure if it was just a term of affection or if he couldn't remember our names. Maybe some of both. When I was in upper elementary school and starting to learn about how our government works, I asked Grandad if he was a Democrat or a Republican. He replied, "Bub, I don't vote for the party; I vote for the man." His words may

READSTOWN

Readstown, February 18—Elmer Groves of Milwaukee was an over Sunday visitor at the home of his father, Fred Groves.

Mrs. Richard Hofland arrived here Saturday evening from Mayville, N. D., for a visit with her mother, Mrs Fred Groves, and other relatives.

Mr. and Mrs. James Maiben received the distressing news Tuesday, of the death of their only grandchild, Ruth Saidy, the nine year old daughter of Mr. and Mrs. Joseph Saidy of Chicago. Deepest sympathy is extended the relatives in the loss of this beautiful child.

Mrs. Sol Townsend is at EauClaire spending a few weeks at the home of her son, Jesse, and family.

Mrs. J. R. Chitwood is at Milwaukee visiting at the home of her son, Carlos.

Jerry O'Leary, James Hill, Avery Anders, were all home for a few days' stay last week from their work at DeSoto.

Olga Heal was hostess to a number of little friends last Thursday afternoon, February 14th, it being the sixth anniversary of her birth.

Mrs. Tillie Watne, of Juanita, N. D., was called here last week on account of the death of her brother, Melvin Anderson.

Austin Crook who is employed in Chicago, is spending a few days with his mother and sisters.

C. H. Carter was a business visitor at Viroqua last week.

N. N. Brigson accompanied his son, Clarence to Milwaukee last week, where he received medical treatment.

Mrs. Grant Smith is confined to her home on account of illness.

C. C. Bennett and family moved to Gotham last Thursday after having resided in this village for a year and one-half, and while here was engaged in the mercantile busines.

Mr. and Mrs. T. J. Crawford entertained a number of friends at Auction bridge last Saturday evening.

Mr. and Mrs. Albert Rosson are the parents of an eight pound baby girl Betty Ann, born Sunday, February 17th.

Mr. and Mrs. Victor Lake and little son of Soldiers Grove were Sunday visitors at the home of his parents, Mr. and Mrs. A. C. Lake.

This column ran in an area newspaper in February 1924. I found the yellowed copy among Mom's papers and realized she had kept it because at the bottom is her birth announcement. Although Grandma Rosson wasn't the Readstown correspondent when this column was written, it is similar to the news she would later write.

be the reason that I have remained an independent voter for the past 50 years.

I thought my grandad was very wise, but his predictions weren't always spot on. In 1961, John F. Kennedy said in his inaugural speech that we would send a man to the moon by the end of the decade. But Grandad said to me, "Mary, if God had meant for men to go to the moon, he would have put them there." He did not live long enough to see the Apollo manned moon landing eight years later.

My grandad was a creature of habit. Every morning he put on his carefully pressed grey cotton work shirt and matching trousers. (He taught me how to iron them, paying special attention to the zipper flap so it would stay flat.) Then he walked uptown. His first stop was at Jones Citco service station where he chatted with the owner, Harlan, and his other cronies. Occasionally, their conversation was interrupted when a car pulled up to the gas pumps. Harlan would fill his customer's tank (gas was 32 cents per gallon), wash the windows, check the oil, take some bills from the driver or add the cost of the fill-up to a running charge account, and then rejoin the conversation.

Grandad's next stop was at the feed store, a block from the service station, and just past the post office. Farmers and retired men from town gathered there daily to swap stories and smoke cigars. His last stop was at the General Store where Grandad would pick up a few grocery items Grandma had written down on a scrap of paper.

Sometimes he would have a small velvet pouch full of pennies he had collected. At the end of each day, Grandad emptied the pockets of his work pants and tossed any pennies he found into a square glass ashtray on top of his dresser. Every so often, he would count the pennies on the kitchen table, grouping them in piles of 10. When he had 100 pennies, he put them in the pouch and traded them at Glass General Store for a silver dollar. Whenever one of his 10 grandchildren celebrated a birthday, they could count on getting a silver dollar from his impressive collection. He gave me 13 silver dollars over the years, which I have since passed on to my grandchildren on their birthdays.

On the morning of June 5, 1967, Grandad made his usual rounds, stopping first at Jones Citco. Hank, the undertaker who lived across the street from the gas station, reported that his dog died during the night. Just like that. No warning. The dog hadn't even been sick. "That's how I want to go," Grandad told the guys. "I don't want to lay around in a hospital. I just want it to be quick and be done with it."

As was his routine, Grandad continued up the block, crossing the street to the feed store where he sat down on a big stack of burlap bags filled with grain and had a heart attack. His obituary says he died in the ambulance on the way to the hospital, but he was probably already gone. Grandad had gotten his wish to go quickly.

My sister, Susan, and I were at school when Grandad died. Toward the end of the school day, the principal's secretary called our names over the intercom asking us to report to the office for a phone call. That rarely happened, so we knew it must be important. It was Mom calling to tell us the sad news. With heavy hearts, we got on the bus for the 10-minute ride home. When the bus doors opened, as we were coming down the steps, a little girl we knew taunted us with, "I know something you don't know!" I was so grateful to Mom for telling us of our beloved grandfather's death before we found out from someone else.

Grandma received sympathy cards in the mail from friends and family members for several weeks after the funeral. Then the day came when she checked her mailbox, and there were no cards. Her eyes filled with tears. We asked her what was wrong and she said, "This is the first day since Albert died that I didn't get at least one card." I've kept that memory with me as a reminder that it's never too late to send a sympathy card.

Grandma Rosson would spend the last quarter of her life without her husband. They had celebrated their 50th wedding anniversary two years earlier. It was observed with a luncheon in the church basement. Little sandwiches, cake, and ice cream squares were served by the church ladies. Grandma and Grandad were in their late 60s then, about the same age I am now, but I remember thinking how very old they seemed.

Grandma and Grandad Rosson on their
45th wedding anniversary in August 1960.

Grandma continued to live in her home for a few years, and then the family decided she should move to senior living. Soon after, we started noticing she sometimes seemed confused. When I helped her put groceries away, I saw that she had six jars of Miracle Whip in the cupboard – more than she could use in a year. It didn't seem like a big thing then, and we all laughed about it.

Once in a while, Grandma would say something to us and stop mid-sentence with a puzzled, troubled look in her eyes. We were very concerned the first time we heard her begin a sentence and finish it with something that sounded like complete gibberish. She looked at us, startled, and said, "That didn't make any sense, did it?"

I was not surprised, only sad, when Mom's sister, Aunt Alice, called to say Grandma couldn't take care of herself anymore and would have to go to a nursing home. The doctors called it "arteriosclerosis" (hardening of the arteries) and "organic brain disease."

After Grandma moved to a nursing home in nearby Soldiers Grove, she wrote letters to me, but her letters were fragmented. It's difficult to read them, not only because her handwriting is shaky and almost illegible, but also because the letters are painful reminders of the devastation the disease had caused.

"I am just wondering what is going to happen to me," she wrote in 1983 when she was 85. "We had a party in the dining room the other day and I got lost. I sat there wondering how I was going to get back. I didn't know I lived in Soldiers Grove. I knew, but I forgot, too..."

She continues the letter, saying she sees people coming into her room. "They have been here all day and won't say a word to me when I talk to them," she wrote. "If I could just hear their voices, I might know where I was. They are carrying a large wicker basket but won't say a word. Please let me know right away if this is all a dream."

Steve and I visited Grandma on a trip home from Tennessee where we were going to college. The nurse was surprised when we told her we were there to see Ellyn Rosson. She warned us Ellyn was "pretty much out of it." I wasn't too concerned – I was sure she'd remember me, her granddaughter. She didn't. Nothing she said made sense. She talked animatedly and cheerfully, but it was word salad. Suddenly, Grandma stopped speaking, looked at Steve, looked back at me, and smiled. Then she said, very clearly, "He looks just like his dad, doesn't he?" For one brief moment, she was the grandma I knew and loved, but then she slipped away again.

The last letter Grandma wrote to me was like the others – mostly rambling nonsensical phrases with names of people I recognized scattered throughout. She closed the letter by writing, "Mary, I wish I could lay down and go to sleep and not wake up, but I guess the Lord takes us when he is ready for us."

On November 23, 1988, at the age of 90, Grandma Rosson went to sleep and didn't wake up. Her daughter, Alice, and her granddaughter, Nancy, stayed with her, gently stroking her face and talking softly to her. Aunt Alice stepped out of the room, just for a minute, and while she was gone, Grandma's shallow breathing stopped. Nancy was at her side. Grandma would finally have the peace she had longed for so many years earlier.

My mom was on the other side of the world when Grandma died. Mom was a thoughtful and attentive daughter, stopping by her mother's house every day before she took a job overseas. Grandma always looked forward to her youngest daughter coming home to Readstown. My mom spent time with Grandma whenever she was back in the country and brought her gifts from all over the world. Grandma would tell me in her letters about Mom taking her to visit friends, to Ladies Aid at church, or out for lunch. She described the gifts Mom brought her – gold jewelry, perfume, a hand-woven basket from Africa.

It's been said that there is a special bond between a grandparent and a grandchild – a kind of intergenerational link that is different than the bond between parent and child. My grandparents, according to most standards, weren't extraordinary. They never graduated from high school, they didn't have any unique talents or abilities, they weren't perfect. But they were special people in my life, and I regret that my children never met my grandad, and they only saw my grandmother as a frail elderly woman whose mind was beginning to leave her.

Perhaps I felt a special connection with my grandparents because I was named after Grandma. Mary Ellen, but with a second "e" instead of a "y." I asked my mom why she didn't name me Mary Ellyn, like Grandma. Mom said she wanted my name to be "correct."

When my daughter was born in 1977, there was no doubt in my mind that her name would be Laura Ellyn, with a "y," like Grandma Rosson spelled her name. Almost twenty-six years later, Laura named her first child, my granddaughter, Anna Ellyn.

Laura Ellyn Steele, 1977

5
Arch Dale McSwain, Jr.

Mom met my dad, Arch Dale McSwain, Jr., in the Army while they were both stationed at Ft. Carson, Aurora, Colorado. Mom was a neuropsychiatric nurse. Mac, as he was known, was a lab technician, born and raised in Paris, Tennessee. They were married in May 1949 in a civil ceremony in Colorado. No family members attended.

To my knowledge, Mom never met Mac's parents. My dad's mother, Rachel Stewart, married his father, Dale McSwain, Sr., in 1919. They had two sons, Mac and his younger brother, Warren. Dale Sr. died of a heart attack at age 42, and after his death, the two boys were separated. Mac was sent to live with other McSwain relatives in Paris. Warren went with their mom to live with Rachel's mother and step-father on a farm outside of Paris. Rachel later developed tuberculosis and spent her last years in a sanitarium.

My mother left the Army shortly after she and my dad were married. They quickly had three children. Susan was born in Virginia where my dad was stationed in 1950, just 11 months after they married. After my dad left the Army they moved to Wisconsin where I was born in 1951, and Michael was born in 1953. Both of my parents worked at the Viroqua hospital, just 10 miles from Readstown where my grandparents lived.

Within a year after Mike was born, our family moved to Florida. I don't know why they left Viroqua after less than two years in Wisconsin. Maybe my dad just missed living in the South. My mom always hated cold weather, so moving to Florida probably seemed like a good idea to her, too.

The marriage was in trouble during our family's time in Florida. My father had a drinking problem, money was tight, and life was difficult. I don't remember much from that time. I was just three or four years old, but I must have understood, at least on a basic level, that our family had serious money problems. I have a clear memory of sitting at a kids' table with Susan, peeling and cutting white potatoes into little pieces using plastic knives. When Mom asked what we were doing, we told her we were going to leave the potato pieces under our pillows for the Tooth Fairy. We knew from experience that the Tooth Fairy gave nickels (sometimes dimes!) for lost teeth, and we thought we could fool her with the potato pieces. It never occurred to us that our little fundraiser was dishonest – we just wanted to help with the family's money problems. Mom explained to us the ethics of trying to fool the Tooth Fairy, and she made us throw away the potato pieces.

My mom told us about one Christmas, probably in 1955 when I was 4½. My parents had arranged gifts for us under the tree – dolls for Susan and me, a football and boy toys for Mike. They were proud of being able to give us nice gifts and knew we'd be excited when we saw them the next morning. Then they remembered I had told them all I wanted for Christmas was raisins. It was Christmas Eve, and the stores were closed. My parents were concerned I would be disappointed despite all the nice gifts under the tree. My dad made a midnight run to the hospital where they both worked and managed to find a single-serving box of raisins in the cafeteria. We weren't indulged as children, and it seemed out of character for my parents to go to the trouble to grant their daughter's wish. I am touched by their effort, but judging from the photos we have from that Christmas, I was pretty happy with my new doll.

Susan, Mike, and me, Christmas 1955

While we were living in Florida, my dad brought home a baby alligator. It was about seven inches long, and we named him Oscar. We thought it was cool to have an alligator for a pet, but then Oscar got too big to keep. I'm not sure what constitutes "too big" for a pet alligator. I think Oscar got to be about a foot long before my parents flushed him down the toilet. But Susan remembers he was about two feet long when my parents released him into a swamp at the end of our street. Neither method of disposing of a pet alligator seems ideal.

I doubt our family did much traveling while in Florida since we were preschoolers and my parents both worked, but I remember walking across the beautiful grounds of the luxurious Fountainebleu Hotel in Miami Beach. What I remember most is the magnificent fountain in front. Susan, Mike, and I were intrigued when we noticed there were hundreds of coins in the fountain. Our parents gave us each a penny and said we could toss it into the fountain and make a wish. They told us if we didn't tell anyone what we wished for it would come true. I was only about four years old, but I distinctly remember wishing that someday I would marry a really nice man. (When my daughter-in-law, Nicole Maria, heard this story she mused that typically little girls would wish for a prince.) My sister kept bugging me to tell her my wish, but I kept it a secret until I married "a really nice man" 16 years later.

My parents' marriage came to an end not long after I found an empty liquor bottle in the bushes by our house, most likely hidden there by my dad. I showed it to my mother, and she was visibly upset. A short time later, Mom loaded her three young children onto a Greyhound bus and made what must have been a long and difficult trip back to Readstown. I have no memory of the day we left or the bus ride, but Susan, who was about five, remembers being car sick and throwing up a good portion of the 1,500-mile trip.

As I grew older, I understood that the topic of my dad was something we didn't talk about. Whenever we broached the subject, Mom would start to tear up. We didn't want to upset her, so we quickly changed the subject. There are so many questions I wish I'd asked her about the breakup. What was the final straw? Did he have a problem with money, perhaps spending it on alcohol? Was he unfaithful? Was he abusive to you? To us? Was he there when we left? If he was, was he sad? What did you tell us was your reason for leaving Florida? Did he try to talk you out of it? Did he ask if he could visit us after the separation? Did the two of you communicate over the years after you left? Did he love you? Did he love us? I'll never know the answers.

I didn't realize until I was much older how difficult it must have been for Mom to swallow her pride and move back in with her parents while she saved enough money for our own place to live. It was the only way she could stretch her salary as a nurse to provide for three young children. Mom would never consider going on public assistance, and I don't think she received child support from my dad. My grandparents helped out by keeping an eye on us kids while she worked.

In 1950s small-town Wisconsin, it must have been humiliating for Mom to tell people her marriage had failed. Grandma Rosson wrote in her weekly news column: "Betty McSwain has moved back to Readstown without her husband." I don't know what prompted Grandma to include that in her news, but I do remember my mom was angry when she saw it in print. It was one of the rare occasions when she verbally expressed her displeasure to her mother. I wish I could remember Grandma's reaction. Was she apologetic? Surprised at Mom's reaction? Mom was always a very private person, and I'm sure she felt a lot of shame in coming back to her hometown "without her husband." Maybe Grandma thought it was an efficient way to get the word out so that Mom (and Grandma?) wouldn't be barraged with questions about her missing husband.

Mom got her job back at the Viroqua hospital. Not surprisingly, raising three young children as a single parent while working full time was stressful for Mom. Adding to the physical and emotional strain was the financial burden of trying to support us on a nurse's salary. Susan, Mike, and I walked on eggshells so as not to upset her. On a bad day, she would fly into a rage over something minor, like not closing the door tightly when the furnace was running, or leaving the lights on when we left a room, or even using too much toilet paper. "Do you think I'm made of money?" she would ask us crossly.

Mom worked at the hospital until 1959 when she received a Public Health Degree from the University of Minnesota and served as the Vernon County Public Health Nurse for nine years. After that, she went back to work at the hospital. She enjoyed her position as the county health nurse, but I think she missed the one-on-one with patients in a hospital atmosphere. She was well-liked and respected at the hospital and in the community. Patients and hospital staff often told us what a good nurse she was.

I ran across one of Mom's performance evaluation forms for 1969-1970 from the hospital in Mom's file box. She was evaluated in ten areas, receiving the highest possible marks in Knowledge of Work, Quality of Work, Attitude toward Work, Initiative, Judgment, Tardiness and Absenteeism, Conduct, and Personal Appearance. The only area in which she didn't get the highest rating was "Attitude Toward Others." Even so, she received the second-highest rating – "Normally Agreeable." I had to smile when I read that. I can confirm that my mom wasn't "Always Agreeable."

Even though we hadn't seen him for several years, my dad and I exchanged a few letters when I was in third or fourth grade. When I wrote to him, he always wrote back. At some point, maybe after a year or two, I stopped writing to him. I'm not sure why. I don't think Mom discouraged us from writing to our dad, and she never spoke badly of him. I wish now I had kept writing and that I had saved his letters.

Our dad came to Readstown once to visit us when we were living with our grandparents. I don't remember much about the visit, but Susan says he brought us presents. He stayed in his car instead of coming into the house, and we went out to the car to see him. That may have been because Grandma and Grandad Rosson would not have been happy to see Mac. I'm guessing they thought their daughter was better off without him.

Sometime in the late 1950s or early '60s, Susan, Mike, and I were playing in our front yard when a car with two men in it drove by slowly and seemed to be watching us. My mom had been looking out the window. She came outside and said, "I think that was your dad." The car went by again in the opposite direction, but it never stopped.

In late October 1962, when I was 11, Mom got a

long-distance call from Florida. On the other end was an administrator from the Fort Walton Beach hospital where my dad worked. She listened quietly, tears slowly running down her face. When she hung up the receiver, she told us our dad had died. He died at home, alone. He had just turned 40 six days before.

An autopsy revealed the cause of death was an "upper gastrointestinal hemorrhage due to esophageal varices due to cirrhosis of the liver," according to the death certificate. It's been called an ugly death. When the varices (lesions) rupture, the first warning is vomiting a large amount of blood, unconsciousness caused by blood loss, and, without medical attention, death. Before that, there are early warning signs, such as an intense itching of the skin, bloating, and a tender, swollen, painful liver and pancreas. He wasn't found until a co-worker from the hospital came to check on my dad after he missed work.

I was sad, partly because my mom was crying, but also because I felt I always loved him. I barely knew my dad, but his death meant I would never be able to fulfill my fantasy of someday finding him and showing him how great I turned out. I was certain he'd be proud of me and sorry for missing out on my childhood. Now he would never know. I realize how unfair it was for me to idolize my dad while criticizing my mom for how she raised us. At least she stuck around and was there for her children.

Although my parents had been separated for five or six years, they weren't divorced until 1961. My dad filed for divorce in Florida, just a year before he died. Decades later, I would learn that he married again shortly after divorcing my mom. The marriage lasted less than a year. If my mom knew he had remarried and divorced again, she never told us.

A few months after his death, Mom received a letter saying she and her children were entitled to his Social Security benefits. It was like a huge weight had been lifted off her shoulders. She wouldn't have to worry so much about money. Mom seemed happier and more relaxed than she'd been in a long time. When we got the first Social Security check, she let Susan and me go to Hazel's Dress & Gift Store by ourselves, and we each got to pick out a new outfit. I don't think we had any store-bought clothes until then. Mom was an excellent seamstress and she made nearly all of our clothing. I still remember the outfit I picked out at Hazel's: an apricot crop-top with matching pedal pushers. Susan picked a similar outfit in light green. We wore our new clothes to a church roller-skating party that night.

That was the only time Mom splurged. She may have spent a small amount of Social Security money on daily needs when her paycheck didn't stretch far enough, but most of it went into a savings account for college. She valued her education and said it had made a big difference for her. At the end of her life, when she was helping us write her obituary, Mom told me, "Mary, without my nursing degree I would have been nothing." It was important that her children had a good education, too.

Of the few things we knew about my dad, one was that he was a very good dancer. In a rare moment when Mom talked about him, she said, "People on the dance floor would stop to watch us dance." She remembered dancing to "The Tennessee Waltz." Mom claimed she wasn't a good dancer, but he made her look good. I think she was being modest.

Another fact I knew about my dad was that he enjoyed photography (as did his father, according to Dale Sr.'s obituary). He entered some pictures of Susan as a baby in an amateur photo contest and won first prize.

I didn't even know what my dad looked like. I vaguely remember dark hair and an average build. The only picture I'd ever seen of him was a small black-and-white snapshot of him standing out in the ocean far from the camera with my brother, Mike, on his shoulders. I would squint to look at it, but I couldn't make out his features. My mom said I had his brown eyes. Hers were blue, my sister's and brother's eyes were green. I felt we had a special connection – my absent dad and me – because our eyes were the same color.

My dad won first prize in a photo contest with this picture of Susan.

By the time I was in high school, all I knew about my dad was that he was a good photographer and a great dancer with a drinking problem. When I was a teenager, I worked up the nerve once to ask Mom, "If you had it to do over again, would you have married him?"

Tears came to her eyes, and after a long pause she said, "Yes."

Did she mean it, or did she give the answer she thought her daughter wanted to hear? Mom dated occasionally, but she never remarried. She was attractive and intelligent, but living in a small town, there weren't many opportunities for a divorced woman in her forties to date. Once she began working overseas, traveling, and meeting new people, she started to date more regularly. I think she may have even gotten a marriage proposal or two. Susan speculates Mom didn't remarry because she'd been hurt once and didn't want to subject herself to that experience again. I'd like to think she didn't marry because our dad was her one true love, but Susan's explanation may be closer to the truth.

When I was in high school, I asked Mom if she

thought she would ever remarry. I was open to the possibility of having a father, or more accurately, a stepfather. She looked at me, hands on her hips, and said, "Mary, why would I want to pick up some man's dirty socks off the floor?"

The only picture I had of my dad during my growing-up years. My brother, Mike, is on his shoulders. Photo taken in 1955.

6
A Good Life

Day 2: December 13, 2008

After the initial shock of the terminal diagnosis, my mother said to Susan and me, "I've had a good life. I've gotten to do things most other people haven't done." That would be her attitude throughout the next 4½ weeks. Mom spent very little time feeling sorry for herself. She was ready to move on to whatever came next, making the entire ordeal seem more like a quiet celebration than a death watch.

We talked about her travels, her friends, and her experiences. We asked Mom if there was anything she wished she'd done or any places she wished she'd visited. A few months previously, she'd signed up for a trip to China sponsored by a local bank, but then suddenly decided to cancel even before she knew she was sick. I asked Mom if she wished she'd spent more of her money on herself. She had always been so frugal. Her main financial goal was saving for a rainy day. Surprised at my question, she looked at me wide-eyed and said, "Mary, I have everything I need."

While sorting through her things after Mom died, I found only old worn dishcloths and tea towels in her kitchen drawer. It made me sad and a little frustrated. All the times we racked our brains trying to think of nice gifts to give her for her birthday or Christmas, when what she needed was a set of new tea towels. I went home that night, reached into a kitchen drawer, and noticed my dish towels were in no better shape than hers. I never thought mine needed to be replaced, so why should she? They were functional. I am my mother's daughter.

I also noticed Mom's worn-looking billfold. Although a good brand, Gucci, it looked like it should have been replaced long ago. Then I remembered that my brother, Mike, had given it to her many years earlier. That explains why she owned a Gucci wallet – she never would have spent that much money on a billfold herself, but Mike would have. It also explains why she didn't replace it. It reminded her of Mike, who died eight years before Mom.

Susan and I asked Mom if she had any regrets. She thought about our question for a while before answering and then said, "No regrets." Despite being married to an alcoholic, separating after a rocky marriage, raising three children alone, her husband dying at age 40, watching her son die, and having three cancer diagnoses, she still was able to say she'd had a good life.

It was very important to Mom that her affairs were in order. She had been preparing for the end of her life for the previous 30 years. All of her financial information was in a white three-ring binder which she asked me to get from her condo and bring back to the hospital. She went over each hand-written entry with us, one by one. Sometimes she expressed concern that we wouldn't understand everything and that we wouldn't be able to carry out her last wishes. We assured her we would, secretly not feeling all that confident. It was difficult to focus on financial matters when our mother was dying, but we tried our best because we knew how important it was to her.

After Mom died, I found a spiral notebook with a page titled "Things I'm Thinking About." It was dated after her hysterectomy but six months before her terminal diagnosis. Written in pencil, she starts with, "If and when necessary." She goes on to list many of the things we talked about at the hospital: where to find her bank statements; names of friends and family to notify of her death; names of contacts to call to cancel her telephone service, newspaper subscription, and auto and health insurance; information about selling her condo, including how much to list it for; where her valuables could be found; a list of her prized possessions to be given to family members; and other notes covering a wide range of personal and business topics.

She also includes end-of-life instructions: "I'd like my ashes to be in the same place as Mike's when convenient. Or any place that's peaceful with lots of birds and animals."

She closes with: "Sorry, you won't find any cash hidden around so don't bother to look!"

*Mom participated in several Relay for Life events,
raising funds for cancer research.*

7
Growing Up

When I was growing up in Readstown, Wisconsin, population 469, the town had three gas stations, a feed store, a funeral parlor, two churches, two restaurants, a dress shop, a hardware store, post office, a furniture store, a bus depot, two grocery stores, a creamery, a barbershop, five taverns, and a tobacco warehouse. There were two main streets which ran north and south. Residents knew them as Front Street and Back Street, but neither had an official name that I was aware of, and there were no street signs or house numbers. There were about a dozen side streets that ran east and west joining Front Street and Back Street. The cemetery was on the west side of town, just beyond the residences, along the river.

Readstown had a K-12 three-story brick school building in the early 1950s, but by the time I was in high school, Readstown High School had been combined with Viola and West Lima High Schools. The merged school was called Kickapoo High School because the Kickapoo River ran through the valley. The river was named for the Kickapoo tribe of Native Americans. A brand-new high school (with a swimming pool!) was built just south of Viola, thanks to a wealthy benefactor.

We lived with Grandma and Grandad Rosson for about two years. By spending frugally and saving every dime she could, Mom was able to buy a brand-new mobile home, and we moved out of our grandparents' house. We were elated the day the trailer arrived and was parked on the empty lot next to the old post office on Front Street. The other kids from the neighborhood came to see our trailer, and we all ran gleefully through the front door, down the hall, and out the back door. We repeated the circuit many more times. We were so proud of our new home. Surprisingly, Mom didn't get mad at us for running through the trailer with our friends. I think she was as excited and happy as we were.

After living in the mobile home for three years, the city offered to buy the lot it was parked on to build a new post office. The trailer was getting small for our family of four, so Mom sold the lot and rented a cute little yellow house behind our trailer. A few years later, after Mom saved up $1,000 for a down payment, she bought the slightly bigger and nicer house next door for $16,500.

When I was four or five, I discovered imaginary friends. That's what Mom called them. I didn't think they were imaginary – they were very real to me. My friends were called Haw-Haws. There were many of them, and they lived in a dark enclosed stairway leading up to an apartment above a tavern in Readstown. The Haw-Haws' bodies looked like empty toilet paper tubes with four legs made out of toothpicks. And they were blue. I don't remember that they talked to me or I talked to them, but I do know I wasn't afraid of the Haw-Haws.

I've learned there are many reasons why children have imaginary friends, and 65% of pre-school through early elementary kids do. Although children can develop imaginary friends as a result of stress or trauma, or because they're lonely, it's far more often the case that imaginary friends grow out of healthy, active imaginations and give children a good way to express their feelings. The latter explanation may have been what my mother thought because I don't remember her being concerned about my imaginary friends. I think she was amused by the colorful and matter-of-fact way I talked about the Haw-Haws. I'd probably have to agree with her assessment because I don't remember feeling lonely as a child.

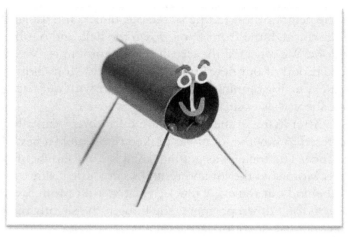

This replica of a Haw-Haw looks just like the ones in my childhood memories.
It was created by Anna, my granddaughter, based on my description.

I had a happy childhood for the most part. I missed my dad, or at least, I missed the idea of having a dad. But I had a sister and brother who were close to me in age, lots of friends, and I liked school. Everyone knew everyone in Readstown. It was an idyllic place for a kid to grow up, nestled between four hills thickly covered with trees in the Kickapoo River Valley.

I realize now that Readstown probably had its share of problems. Poverty was perhaps the most obvious one. Many residents worked at the tobacco warehouse or raised tobacco themselves, and others were dairy farmers or worked at the creamery. There were few employment opportunities in Readstown, so some residents commuted to Viroqua to work at businesses or for the city or county. Business owners and professionals were generally better off, but I don't know of anyone who would have been considered wealthy.

Alcoholism was likely a problem since there were five taverns in a town of 469. I remember the bars being as busy during the day as in the evening. My great-uncle Floyd and great-aunt Rubie ran one of the taverns. I often went into their bar with my cousin (their granddaughter) and watched the regular customers play cards. Aunt Rubie taught my cousin and me at an early age to play Canasta, 500, Euchre, and other card games.

Physical abuse existed in some homes, in part because it was common for parental discipline to include spankings and, in some families, beatings with a stick or belt. I wasn't aware of abuse in my friends' families, but I had a front-row seat for a horrible incident of abuse that took place in my 5th-grade classroom.

We had a teacher who was physically and emotionally abusive. He would pick on a few students, usually boys. Once, the teacher punished a classmate for chasing girls with a dead mouse at recess and made him sit for the rest of the day with the dead mouse on his desk. That was after the teacher kicked the boy from desk to desk, forcing the poor kid to apologize to every student. All the while, he yelled insults at the boy. The ranting went on for hours. It was traumatizing for the boy, of course, but also for the other students.

I told Mom what had happened when I got home from school. She was appalled and angry. She said the teacher was mentally ill. It was the only time my mom called a school administrator to criticize a teacher. Unfortunately, that sadistic teacher was still teaching at Readstown years later. It was probably difficult to recruit teachers to move to a small town with low pay.

We didn't have much money, but none of my friends' families did either. Very few homes had televisions – we didn't get one until I was in 5th grade. Sometimes on summer mornings, Susan, Mike, and I went to Grandma's and Grandad's house. We would watch the test pattern on their black-and-white TV until the first show came on. I think it was "I Love Lucy." In the evenings, we sometimes got to watch "The Ed Sullivan Show," "Lassie," and "Mr. Ed." My grandparents only got one channel, and we would frequently have to manipulate the rabbit-ears antenna to get a slightly less fuzzy picture. We wrapped a piece of tin foil around the antenna, and occasionally it helped.

We often played school with our cousins, Nancy and Annette, in their walk-out basement and entertained ourselves with jewelry swaps. We collected our moms' hand-me-down costume jewelry and traded the pieces among the four of us. Each piece changed hands several times over the summer.

My first day of first grade in August 1957 with Susan and my cousin Nancy.

Fifty-some years later, when I had two young granddaughters, I got out all the cast-off costume jewelry Mom and I had collected over the years. I excitedly gave the jewelry to Anna and Ally to play with. I told them about the jewelry swaps that my cousins, my sister, and I had when we were kids. The girls were very polite, picking up some of the pieces, looking at them and then at each other genuinely confused, as if to say, "What do we do with these?" It was clear I had overestimated the entertainment value of trading old cheap jewelry. In the age of dolls that look like their owners, video games, and organized kids' sports, jewelry swaps probably seem a little mundane.

Living in a small town without a theater, a roller-skating rink, or shopping malls meant we had to create our own entertainment. Our backyard bordered the backyards of several of our friends' lawns. In the summer, we spent many happy hours in the open grassy space playing Kick-the-Can, Starlight Starbright, and Hide-and-Seek until long after dark. When playing alone or with a sibling or friend, we'd play marbles, jump rope, or jacks. We created tents for playhouses using blankets spread over a picnic table or clotheslines, held in place by clothespins which were also used as stakes.

We played Annie, Annie Over with neighbor kids and our cousins, throwing a ball over Grandad's washhouse. The washhouse was a small building in the backyard where he kept his tools and where Grandad and Grandma did the laundry every week. On wash day, the kids had the job of carrying clean water from the house to the washhouse, pouring it into the wringer washer and rinse tub. After the clothes were washed, rinsed, and hung on the clothesline to dry, we dumped the buckets of dirty water into the ditch at the back of my grandparents' yard.

When we outgrew kids' games, we played cards in our neighbor's clubhouse. We rode our bikes, carrying our sparse fishing gear, to the river. We started with bamboo poles and then graduated to rods and reels as we got more experienced. We never caught much except for small bullheads and catfish which we threw back into the murky water.

All the neighborhood kids spent a good part of every summer day at Tree Town. That was the name we gave to a cluster of treehouses nestled in the crooks and branches of trees along a cow path halfway up the hill behind our house. We carried a hodgepodge of construction materials to Tree Town — scrap boards, hand saws, nails, duct tape, and hammers. Using our imaginations, we cobbled together rustic treehouses or built additions onto ones already there. We borrowed furnishings like old rugs, blankets, and plastic dishes from our parents (or smuggled them out of the house). If our treehouses were perched high enough in the trees, we could see all of Readstown, from the Kickapoo River to

41

uptown. We spent countless hours at Tree Town, hiking back down the hill only when our parents hollered or whistled for us to come home for meals and bedtime.

Mom had these 1959 school pictures of Susan, Mike, and me in this frame on her dresser for as long as I can remember.

In the winter, we hauled our sleds and saucers up the Tree Town hill, around to the northeast where trees and brush had been cleared for a new elementary school and play area. It was a steep slope, ideal for sledding, and most winter days the hill was covered with at least a foot of snow. The top layer sometimes melted in the sun and froze again as night fell. It made for a fast, bumpy, and challenging ride.

It was not unusual for kids to lose control and go flying off the sled, hitting the icy snow, which sometimes resulted in large goose eggs on their heads. We took turns pulling the injured friend (or friends) home on a toboggan. All the while, the kid would ask, "Where am I?" What happened? Where are we going?" We would answer the questions, and then they would repeat the same series of questions. We were relieved to find out this scary behavior was the result of a concussion and not some kind of sudden-onset juvenile mental illness. Rarely was anyone taken to the ER, but often my mom, the only nurse in town, was consulted. There were no doctors in Readstown, and the closest hospital was 10 miles away.

Readstown was unique for a small town in that it offered a free show every Wednesday night in the summer at the city park. Local business people provided funds to string up a white screen, purchase a projector, and show old movies once it got dark. Kids sat on blankets while watching the show, and young lovers took the opportunity to make out under the blankets. Popcorn was available to purchase for 10 cents a bag (15 cents with extra butter) at the tiny concession stand, just big enough for one person to pop popcorn and make change. People came to Readstown from nearby towns and rural areas on free-show night. It was a good opportunity for farm families to do their shopping and take care of other business while their kids were happily occupied at the free show with friends. On Thursday mornings, we'd go back to the park to look for coins that might have fallen out of pockets during the movie.

My friend, Debbie, lived across the side street from the funeral home. We could watch the comings and goings at the funeral home from the swing set in her backyard. Every week or two, the hearse would bring a body for embalming and visitation. Sometimes we'd see trucks delivering caskets and vaults.

Our friend, Hanky, lived with his parents in the top floor apartment in a big white Queen Anne-style house on Front Street. The main floor of the house was the funeral parlor, and Hanky's dad, Hank, was the undertaker. The inside of the funeral parlor was as dark and dim as the outside was white and stately. Maroon velvet draped the windows and kept out any rays of sunshine that vainly tried to penetrate the darkness, typical of most funeral homes in the 1950s. The only light came from a goose-necked brass lamp attached to the walnut podium which held the guest book and a floor lamp with a burgundy shade near the casket viewing area.

Sometimes a few of us kids would talk Hanky into sneaking us into the funeral parlor when a body was laid out for viewing. Filled with both anticipation and terror, we would cautiously approach the satin-lined coffin. The body was usually that of an older person with makeup applied more generously than fashionably. We'd stand very still, holding our breath, watching for some sign of life – a slight rising of the chest or flicker of the eyelid.

I don't remember any of the bodies specifically, except for one: a baby, or maybe a toddler, wearing corduroy overalls and white baby shoes. She looked like she was sleeping.

My unauthorized visits to the funeral home were exciting, but also sobering. I've been asked if those visits shaped or changed my attitude about death. It's hard to say. As I grew older and started attending funerals of people I knew, someone would invariably ask, "Didn't he look good?" To which I silently replied, "No, he looked dead." One thing I knew for sure: I did not want to be on display when I died. I hated the thought of viewers commenting on how good (or how bad) I looked.

The highlight of my summer was attending church camp in northern Wisconsin about 150 miles north of Readstown. I went every year from 3rd grade through high school. I would start a list of "Things I Need to Take to Camp" months in advance, and I would start packing three or four weeks before my departure date slowly rolled around.

One memorable camp experience was the snipe hunt. Campers were told we needed to take a pillowcase to use as a bag to catch the snipe. When it was dark, the camp counselors took us out into a forested area beyond the cabins. We were given a vague description of what snipe look like. The leaders instructed us to call, "Here snipe, here snipe." We were so intent on looking for snipe, we barely noticed the staff had disappeared. After what seemed like hours, and without finding a single snipe, we began to get suspicious. The camp counselors eventually came back to tell us the snipe hunt was a hoax.

When I was too old to be a camper, I continued going to camp for several years, volunteering as a cabin mom and kitchen helper. I also taught classes. One of those classes was

"Conversational Prayer," based on the book by Rosalind Rinker. What I learned from leading the class has stayed with me for the past 50 years. I discovered that prayer could and should be like having a conversation with God that begins when I wake up in the morning, continues periodically all day, and doesn't end until I lie down to sleep at night. Only then do I say "Amen."

Despite the mostly happy times, I felt like there was a dark cloud over my head throughout my childhood and even into adulthood. I was the only kid in my class whose parents were divorced or separated. In second grade, we made ashtrays out of clay to give to our dads for Father's Day. I didn't have a father to give it to. Miss Carter, my very special classroom teacher who was also my Sunday School teacher, sensed my discomfort and quietly suggested I give it to my grandad. He was like a father to me, and as a long-time cigar and pipe smoker, he would make good use of it.

In her memoir, *The Shadow Man: A Daughter's Search for Her Father,* author Mary Gordon says, "A fatherless child thinks all things are possible, but nothing is safe." I identify with that. I consider myself to be a mix of realist and optimist, but in the back of my mind, I am waiting for the other shoe to drop. My life seems almost perfect now, but I wonder if it will continue to be. I'm open to new experiences, but I'm leery about how they might turn out. I think all parents and grandparents worry about the health and safety of their children and grandchildren, but my anxiety became more intense and persistent as I dealt with my mother's illness and after her death. I desperately wanted a guarantee that my family would be protected.

When I was young, I thought I was psychic. I felt I knew things that no one had told me – I just knew. I thought being psychic made me special. Now I realize what a terrible burden it would be to see the future, to know something awful is going to happen in five years or ten years, and to carry around that knowledge without being able to change the outcome. I've decided that not knowing the future is better.

8
Best Friends

My happy childhood was in large part because I had a best friend. Debbie Olson was the oldest of four girls. When her unmarried aunt had a baby boy, Debbie's parents adopted him, completing their family. Debbie lived kitty-corner across the backyard from our house. We developed a high-pitched ear-piercing scream that sounded more like a whistle: *EEERRR-REEET*! It was how we called each other to come out and play. I've tried, but I can't make that sound anymore.

I was always a little in awe of Debbie. She had olive skin, pretty brown eyes, and long dark hair which her mother painstakingly curled into ringlets when she was little. Once, we almost missed the bus to go swimming because her mom wasn't done curling her hair. For swimming! I, on the other hand, was plain and chubby ("pleasingly plump," my grandad would say). I had strawberry blond hair, freckles, and a part between my front teeth. I used to think how lucky I was that this beautiful girl – certainly destined to be Miss America someday – wanted to be my friend.

In addition to being pretty, Debbie was also talented. She was an accomplished pianist by the age of 14. Her mom made her practice the piano every day to the annoying tick of a timer that would buzz when her requisite 30 minutes were up. I spent countless hours sitting next to Debbie on the uncomfortable oak piano bench waiting for her to finish so we could go out and play. Sometimes I helped the time pass more quickly by forcing the dial ahead. Not too much, just a minute or two, or her mom would get suspicious, march into the room, and turn the dial back to 30. Debbie would have to start over, further delaying our playtime.

My mom didn't like for us to have friends in the house when she got home from work. She would say, "I have to be nice to people all day long. I don't want to have to be nice when I come home." So I spent a lot of time outside with friends and at Debbie's house. With five kids in her family, one more didn't make much difference. Her dad was funny and nice. Although I was painfully bashful around adult males, I liked him. Looking back, I realize he became something of a father figure for me.

Like other Readstown kids, Debbie and I spent a lot of time at Tree Town in the summer and sledding in the winter. We rode our bikes all around town, often ending up at the cemetery reading the headstones. When we weren't riding bikes, we roller skated on metal skates that clipped to our tennis shoes, using a special key to tighten them.

Debbie and I were always dreaming up new ideas to keep us entertained. After reading stories about Laura Ingalls Wilder, we decided to make maple syrup. We planned to use it on pancakes, but we also wanted to try pouring hot syrup onto the snow so it would turn into a taffy-like candy. At least, that's what Laura Ingalls Wilder said would happen.

We drove spikes into the maple trees in Debbie's yard, hung buckets on the spikes, and soon we had pails full of sap. We carried the buckets into Debbie's basement and started boiling it. We didn't know that it takes 40 gallons of sap to make one gallon of syrup. We boiled for hours, but finally gave up. By the time we decided to scrap the project, we had several pails full of sap which began to look and smell awful. It turns out maple sap has a shelf life about the same

*Debbie (dark hair, center) and me (right) at our 8th-grade graduation.
Other classmates are Leanne Granger, Terry Nelson, and Lou Ann Nelson.*

as milk – a fact we didn't know when we started the project.

One summer, when Debbie and I were in 6th or 7th grade, we decided to make a raft. Like the maple syrup scheme, we were inspired by a book we'd read in school. Kon-Tiki, written by Thor Heyerdahl, is based on his three-month voyage across the Pacific Ocean on a raft. We called our raft the Kon-Tiki II. We borrowed two oil barrels from Debbie's dad, who owned the local hardware store and drove the Standard Oil truck. We attached the barrels to the underside of a platform we'd banged together out of used pieces of wood and a cast-off wooden ironing board. We added a flagpole and flag, and after a few days of construction, it was ready to sail. Or so we thought.

We convinced Debbie's dad to load the monstrosity into the back of his truck and haul it to the Manning Slough, a marshy pond on the north edge of town. It seemed like half of the community, kids and adults, came to watch our maiden voyage and cheer us on. Everyone helped get the Kon-Tiki II into the water, and it floated beautifully. We christened it with a bottle of Coke, which never did break, and then smugly climbed aboard.

For one brief moment, perched high above the water on the floating oil barrels, we reveled in our remarkable accomplishment. Then our weight shifted slightly, and the Kon-Tiki II suddenly flipped over, throwing us fully clothed into the water. (We were so confident in the raft's seaworthiness it never occurred to us to wear swimsuits.) Coming up sputtering, we were appalled to see everyone on the shore laughing hysterically.

The onlookers thought it was the best entertainment they'd had in a long time. Debbie and I didn't find it at all humorous. We stood in waist-deep water, with the Kon-Tiki II floating upside down behind us, oil barrels to the sun. We had to admit we looked ridiculous. Once we got over our initial disappointment, we decided to go swimming since we were already wet. The kids watching from the shore jumped in with us, also in street clothes, and we all enjoyed a memorable afternoon of swimming and water fights.

Ice skating became a favorite winter activity for Readstown kids after Debbie, Susan, and I spearheaded a fundraiser to create an ice rink. We came up with the idea of selling canning jars, which everyone had on shelves in their basements and used them to store produce from their gardens. We asked for donations of jars, placed them in a wagon, and pulled it from door to door. Residents were gracious enough to donate or buy the jars. Some did both.

I don't know how many jars we sold, but at five cents each, it couldn't have been enough to pay for the upkeep of the skating rink. I think community leaders were impressed with our effort, however, because that winter and every winter thereafter, we had a flooded field on which to skate. We would build a fire using old tires and whatever other combustible materials we could find. We'd skate for hours, coming home only when we were too frozen to move our fingers and toes, our faces frostbitten, and our bodies sore from frequent falls.

Debbie and I earned spending money by picking

Fruit Jar Sellers Started Skating Rink

"If you want a thing well done, you must do it yourself." So goes the old saying. This, apparently, was the feeling of Susan McSwain, daughter of Mrs. Betty McSwain and Debra Olson, daughter of Mr. and Mrs. Lawrence Olson as they started out last summer selling fruit jars. The girls wanted an ice-skating rink this winter and decided if they started a fund maybe some of the grown-ups would pitch in and help. To date the girls have $11.60 in their fund.

How about it folks? The ice-skating season will soon be here.

The Advancement Association plans to bring it up at their next meeting Tuesday, November 1, so why not be there. Let's give the youngsters a hand with their project.

Debbie and Susan had their picture taken for the Oct. 23, 1960 Readstown
Special along with a front-page story about our skating rink fundraising project.
I don't remember why I wasn't included in the photo or article, but
I'm sure I wasn't happy about the slight.

strawberries and apples at orchards around nearby Gays Mills. We also babysat, earning 50 cents an hour, regardless of the number of children in the family.

By the time we were in high school, Debbie had become a beautiful, popular young woman. She was a cheerleader, class officer, and pianist for the school choir. She could have dated any of the boys at Kickapoo High School. She chose a good student and athlete who was liked by everyone.

Debbie and her boyfriend went their separate ways when her family sold the hardware store and moved to Milwaukee during her junior year. She wasn't happy about missing her last two years at KHS. Our class, the Class of '69, was a close-knit group, and that made it hard for her to leave her friends, many of whom she'd had since first grade. Her parents tried to sweeten the deal by buying her a baby grand piano which helped ease her disappointment.

I spent a summer with Debbie after graduation. The plan was to be nannies for wealthy families in Chicago, but our employment lasted only two weeks. We decided we weren't ready to take over the raising of someone else's children. Instead, we moved in with Debbie's family, and we got jobs cleaning rooms at the Milwaukee YMCA.

In the fall, I left for college in Nebraska. Debbie and I wrote regularly since calling long distance was too expensive. Two years later, at weddings three weeks apart, we walked down the aisle as each other's bridesmaids. I married Steven

Debbie on her wedding day. Her sister
Mary (center) and I were bridesmaids.

Steele, who I met at college, and Debbie married a handsome young police officer who adored her. Their marriage didn't last long – I'm not sure why. Debbie and I started to lose touch after that. She remarried and had a baby boy. I sent her birth announcements when each of our three children were born, and we exchanged Christmas cards for a few years. Those years were a blur of diapers, sippy cups, and preschoolers for me, and we lost track of each other. But I thought about her often.

On Christmas Eve in 1986, I impulsively called directory assistance for Milwaukee in an effort to contact Debbie. It was easy to find her phone number because she was using her maiden name. I dialed the number. When she answered, her voice sounded the same, but more serious, more mature. She told me about her young son, her husband, and her plans to have another child. I wished her a Merry Christmas and hung up the phone. It was the last time I would hear her voice.

On Friday, April 14, 1989, I was getting ready for my first day at my new job at Iowa Lakes Community College when the phone rang. I hesitated before answering the phone because I didn't want to be late for work. I decided I had a little time, so I picked up the receiver. I heard a voice at the other end say, "Mary, this is Karen. I'm afraid I have some bad news."

Karen didn't say her last name, but after a few moments, I realized it was Debbie's youngest sister. It had been about 20 years since I last talked to her. Debbie died during the night, Karen said, just 10 days before her 38th birthday. She had gotten up with her young son who was crying, and she laid down in his bed so he would go back to sleep. Her husband found her in the morning, not breathing, still cradling the sleeping child. They didn't know the cause of death. "Her heart just stopped," Karen said. There would be an autopsy. The funeral would be Monday in Readstown.

On Sunday morning, Steve and I made the five-hour trip to Readstown where the funeral would be held. My childhood friend, Hanky, having taken over the business from his father, greeted us solemnly at the door of the funeral home. Now using his given name, John Henry spoke with us quietly for a few minutes in the foyer. We talked about Debbie and our shared childhood. He told me about bringing her back to Readstown from Milwaukee in the silver and black hearse. An oldies show was playing on the radio, and he said he listened to our generation's favorite songs from the '60s and '70s all the way home. He said it was an emotional and surreal experience.

Walking into the viewing room, still decorated in maroon velvet, brought back the feelings of anticipation and dread from my childhood visits to this place. Near the casket, there were pictures of Debbie at the piano, in her high school cheerleading uniform, with her family. I took a deep breath and moved closer to the casket. I hadn't seen Debbie in 15 years or more, and I felt like I was looking at a vaguely familiar stranger.

I had forgotten that she was my age, almost 38, and not 18 anymore. There were unexpected wrinkles around her eyes and a crease between her eyebrows. It puzzled me, that deep crease. Then I remembered how the furrow would appear when she concentrated on a difficult piano piece or when she was annoyed with her sisters. But the wrinkle would quickly disappear when she smiled. Sometime over the past 20 years, the line had become permanent. What bothered me more than the wrinkles was her hair. It didn't look right. It was short and kind of curly, a style an older person might wear. Debbie's dark hair was always long, straight, and shiny.

The white azalea plant I had ordered was near the casket next to a beautiful bouquet of red roses. I looked at the card on the bouquet – it was from her high school boyfriend. I was surprised and touched by the gesture. I guess after all these years, Debbie was still a part of his thoughts, or at least, his memories.

I left a long note for Debbie's family, telling them I was sorry I wouldn't be able to attend the funeral the next day. I explained that I couldn't miss my second day at my new job. But, truthfully, I didn't think I could bear facing the family's grief – or mine. I looked at Debbie one last time, said good-bye to John Henry, and headed back to Iowa.

Debbie's family didn't contact me after the funeral. I've often wondered why they didn't reply to the note I left. Perhaps it was too difficult for them. Maybe they thought I should have been at the funeral. I think about Debbie often, and sometimes I dream about her. She's always young and healthy in my dreams, and she's still 18.

The death certificate indicated Debbie died of meningitis, according to one family member. There were various rumors about other possible causes. But Karen's simple explanation when she called to tell me Debbie had died is all I need to know: "Her heart just stopped."

In the end, that's what happens to all of us.

Debra Jean Olson, 1951-1989

9
A Good Death

Because she'd been a nurse for four decades, Mom felt comfortable in a hospital setting. She seemed to enjoy visits by the doctors, nurses, and aides who monitored her IV pain medication, straightened her bedding, and took her for baths. Her pain was being managed, and we all agreed it was best for her to stay in the hospital.

Mom's doctor, however, said there would come a time when Medicare would no longer pay for her hospital stay. We told him when that time came, we'd pay. It was worth any amount of money to ensure she continued to receive the excellent care she was getting in the hospital. He suggested we talk with hospice staff in case we changed our minds.

On the seventh day at the hospital, the hospice director came to Mom's room to let us know about hospice services. One goal of hospice is for the patient to have "a good death," defined as freedom from pain, retention of control, comfort, as much autonomy and independence as possible, retaining dignity, the presence of people the patient cares about and who care about the patient, and being treated with compassion and respect.

The goals of hospice correlate closely with the fears that patients with a terminal illness have:

1. Fear of pain and physical suffering.
2. Fear of being lonely or dying alone.
3. Fear of what will become of loved ones.
4. Fear of being a burden.
5. Fear of dying without peace, resolution, forgiveness.
6. Fear of loss of control.
7. Fear of the unknown – and death is the ultimate unknown.
8. Fear of being forgotten.

The hospice staff told us Mom couldn't be admitted to hospice unless she was first dismissed from the hospital. We didn't anticipate that Mom would be dismissed and so she wouldn't qualify for hospice services. But it was comforting to know help would be available to us if and when needed.

Hospice Notes: *Met with patient, two daughters, and son-in-law and explained hospice and services. Answered their questions about when hospice could admit (after discharge). In the meantime, we could provide support and answer their questions. The patient is knowledgeable about her care and prognosis, as well as family. She is very satisfied with pain management at this time. I gave them publications "Gone from my Sight" and "Signs and Symptoms of End of Life." Spiritual care is being provided, and family has strong faith.*

They had questions about admitting patient to hospice while in the hospital. I reviewed with them our regulations of needing hospital to discharge before admission to hospice. They verbalized that they didn't want to "mess with what is working now," as the patient is comfortable with the IV and PCA (patient-controlled analgesia for pain). *Hospice will offer support and guidance as needed. All were very appreciative of hospice efforts and information.*

10
Happy, Healthy Kids

Although I knew my mom loved us, and we loved her, I grew up feeling I could never please her. In retrospect, I think she was proud of us but just unable to express it. I rarely remember her telling us she loved us when we were young. Physical affection was not often shared by Mom either. When I was seven or eight, I had strep throat and Mom was worried, concerned that I might be developing scarlet fever. She comforted me by rubbing my back as I lay across her lap. Sixty years later, I still remember how good it felt to be touched by her.

Another thing I remember about Mom is that she didn't like being in debt to anyone. If we needed something from Glass General Store while she was at work, we would charge a half-gallon of milk for our cereal or big bologna for sandwiches. When she came home from work and we told her we had charged something, she would immediately send one of us to the store with cash to pay off the bill. To my knowledge, Mom never bought anything on credit except our house and a 1957 Ford Fairlane which she needed to get to work after returning to Readstown with her children on the bus. Her disdain for debt, and her reluctance to spend money, is probably the reason she was able to buy a car, a house, and pay for her children's college education.

Even though money wasn't quite as tight going into our high school years, life was still a struggle for Mom. She could be very demanding, anxious, and unhappy. She would get angry over some small thing we'd done – or not done. Once she was so upset with Susan and me, she told us to leave the house. I don't remember what the offense was, but I clearly remember the consequences. We were young teens, and we didn't know where to go, so we went to Debbie's house. I'm sure her parents wondered why we were there after 8 p.m., but they welcomed us into their home. After an hour or so, we decided to see if it was safe to go back to our house. Mom had calmed down and may have been worried about us being out after dark. I think Susan thought it was a great adventure, but I was troubled that Mom told us to leave.

When I was about 10, I wrote a list of things I would never do when I became a mom: I'd never yell at my children, say anything that would make them feel bad, expect them to act like adults when they were only kids, or spank them. I would take their glasses to school when they forgot them at home.

The list was much longer, but those are the key points. (My kids would attest to the fact that I didn't always follow through on those lofty goals.) Usually, there was a common theme with Mom's blow-ups: We weren't appreciative enough of her hard work. I don't think many children are able to appreciate the physical and emotional toll parenting can take until they become parents themselves.

Susan, Mike, and I tried not to upset Mom, especially when she was in a bad mood. In an effort to make her happy, we'd do things we thought – hoped – would put her in a good mood: clean our rooms, do the laundry in the old wringer washer and hang it up on the clothesline, have supper ready when she got home from work. It always seemed to cheer her when we all pitched in, trying to make her life a little easier.

We also found we could make her smile by writing cute little poems for her. I'd almost forgotten them until I found several tucked away in her metal box where she kept her valuables and important papers. Here's one we wrote for Mother's Day when Susan, Mike, and I were in high school:

To Mother, May 12, 1968

Sunday is that special day
That comes just once a year,
The day we honor Mother
And fill her day with cheer.

But how could we be cheerful?
It wasn't very funny —
We wanted to give you something special,
But none of us had money.

What could we give on Mothers' Day?
We thought and thought for hours.
We couldn't buy a present;
We couldn't send you flowers.

We couldn't take you to a show,
Not even out to dinner.
Though you're getting awfully slim,
Our pocketbooks are slimmer.

Then we knew just what you wanted
More than pots or pans or lids,
We're giving you what you always asked for:
Three happy, healthy kids!

Whenever we asked Mom what she wanted for Mothers' Day, her birthday, or Christmas, she always gave us the same answer: "I want happy, healthy kids." When we pressed her, she'd say she could always use more bobby pins. Bobby pins were less than a dollar, so we bought them at the General Store and wrapped them up. As we got older and had slightly bigger budgets for gifts, we gave her Evening in Paris perfume and Yardley soap, two of her favorite things.

I found another poem I wrote with a different purpose in mind. This one was to put her in a good mood with the goal of convincing her to make me a new outfit for a special school event, the annual talent show:

Dear Mom,

> *Friday is the talent show,*
> *A great event, no less.*
> *And I think that you should know*
> *I haven't got a dress.*

> *I know I ask a lot of you,*
> *But may I please ask one thing more —*
> *I want so much something new,*
> *Although I am very poor.*

> *A black dress would look so nice*
> *On your lovely daughter, brown eyes alive,*
> *Whipped cream crepe will suffice*
> *Made from Butterick pattern five, two, two, five.*

> *For these things, from my allowance, I will pay*
> *And for this dress you sew*
> *I will thank you more than I can say*
> *And be the prettiest girl at the talent show!*

Love and Kisses,
Mary

I don't remember ever having a black dress, but I'm pretty sure she made me a new outfit. I'm guessing she decided another color would be better for me than black. What I wanted often took a back seat to what Mom thought was best for me.

My mom could be very loving and thoughtful, and though she didn't often express it verbally, she showed it in other ways. When her kids were sick, Mom couldn't afford to stay home with us and miss work. Instead, she made the 20-mile round-trip home to Readstown from the Viroqua hospital over her lunch break to check on us. After Susan and I both had our tonsils out on the same day and weren't able to eat solid foods, Mom brought us malts. That was a special treat, as Mom normally wouldn't have wasted money on fast food.

One year, Mom knitted beautiful V-neck mohair sweaters for Susan and me for Christmas. Susan's was green and mine was red. She wanted them to be a surprise and so she could only knit after we'd gone to bed. As the Christmas deadline approached, she took them to work with her and knitted over her noon hour.

When Susan and I were at college, Mom sent cookies and wrote letters, sometimes with cash tucked inside. She occasionally tried her hand at poetry. I found a homemade valentine card that she sent when I was in college. It was decorated with valentines – some drawn by her as well as cutouts of children's valentine cards pasted on a piece of typing paper. The only text on it was in her handwriting with a red marker:

> *Roses are red,*
> *Violets are blue,*
> *Don't write any more checks,*
> *You're long overdrew!*

She sent a check along with her homemade valentine to cover my overdraft. Reading it now, 50 years later, I am reminded that she had a sense of humor.

Mom's homemade valentine.

11
Don't Borrow Trouble

Day 8: December 19, 2008

Although Mom seemed content at the hospital, she expressed concern about her savings being spent on her care. "I don't want all my money to go to the government," she said firmly. We're not sure why she thought the money would go to the government instead of to the hospital. Mom had always been frugal, but this was the first sign of an obsession with money that would increase as she became more ill.

The days were often long and stressful for me. I would arrive at the hospital around 8 a.m. and stay until 8 p.m. The days were even longer for Susan. She stayed night and day in Mom's hospital room, leaving only to get a meal in the hospital cafeteria. Susan said she preferred being there 24/7 and that being with Mom *relieved* her stress. It was clear that of the two of us, she was the more natural caregiver.

I felt as if I was falling apart sometimes. I was afraid I wouldn't be able to get through what lay ahead of us. I was blessed to have the support of friends and family.

My friend, Jane, who lost both her parents to cancer, understood my anxiety and sent me this beautiful email:

Dec. 19, 2008

I know you didn't ask for advice, Mary, but I'm providing some, anyway. (You aren't surprised, are you?) Use it or ignore it, as you choose.

Don't borrow trouble. Live in the moment. If your mother is feeling OK today, enjoy it without worrying about what tomorrow or the next day is going to bring. Lots of what you worry about will not happen or be an issue, so don't taint the blessings of today worrying about what might — or might not — come next.

With my parents, I felt almost paralyzed with fear sometimes about whether I would be able to handle him or her getting really bad, whether it would be worse to actually be with them when they died — or to not be with them when they died, how long I could be gone from work, etc. A lot of that stuff was never an issue, except that I made it an issue when I spent time and energy worrying about it needlessly. You will deal with whatever you have to deal with when/if it happens. Don't borrow trouble. Enjoy the blessings of the moment.

It is a blessing and privilege to be able to be there for a parent at the end of her life. You will never regret any of this time that you spend with your mother over the next few days, weeks, or months. Say what you need to say. That may include:

"I love you."

"One thing I've always admired about you is …."

"Talk to me about your mother." (Or your Mom's father. Or your father.)

"Knowing how tough it was for Steve and me to take care of and support three kids, I can't believe that you were able to do it so well as a single parent. What was the hardest part or time period?"

"Were you scared when you left for Saudi Arabia?"

"Do you think I'm more like you or like my father?"

"Are you scared?"

I love you, Mary, and I know how much your mother loves you. She's very lucky to have you and Susan and your families close by, and you're very lucky to be able to be there for her at the end of her life. Your Mom didn't move to Spencer because of the housing or medical care available here. She moved here because you and Steve and the kids were here... Let me know if there is anything you need.

Love, Jane

Jane ends with a P.S., and in true Midwest tradition she adds, "I'll bring over two pans of lasagna, one for you and Steve and one for your freezer."

I still treasure the message. What a gift to be able to say just the right words to a friend who is hurting.

12
Brazil

My mother was a world-class worrier. She worried about little things and big things equally. She never let her gas tank get below half full for fear of running out of gas, a habit she continued all her life. If Susan was even a few minutes late getting home from a date, Mom would nervously pace through the house, repeating her usual line: "She could be in a ditch somewhere!" Having witnessed Mom's extreme anxiety first hand, I made it a point never to be late. I also learned to be anxious, especially regarding my family's health and safety.

Mom had reasons to be worried about her children's safety. While I was in high school, there were three accidents on the curvy, hilly roads throughout the Kickapoo Valley that took the lives of three classmates. One was a student named Mike who was riding with his family to the graduation ceremony. His car was hit head-on by another car carrying other students who had turned around because they'd forgotten something at home. I was riding in the car following Mike's vehicle. I saw the EMTs attending to passengers who were visibly injured. Mike didn't appear to be hurt except there was blood coming from one ear. He died later from a brain bleed. He was 16. Two other students we knew well were killed in separate accidents while out late at night with friends.

Despite Mom's anxiety about her children, she encouraged me to compete for one of two positions as a foreign exchange student during my senior year of high school. If chosen, it would be a wonderful experience for me to travel to a part of the world I might not otherwise see. I think Mom's desire for me to travel outweighed the fact that she would worry every day I was gone. I was selected by teachers and the student council to be one of Kickapoo High School's exchange students, along with my friend, Hanky. Our fellow classmates sold candy bars to pay for our expenses.

The original plan was for me to go to Hawaii. Because it was a state with many different cultures, it was on the list of potential destinations from which I could choose. I would live with a Pacific Islander family. For some unknown reason, the placement in Hawaii fell through about three weeks before I was scheduled to leave. I got a call from a staffer at the organization that set up placements for American students. The woman asked me, "Mary, how would you like to go to Rio?" I had no idea where Rio was, but I told her it sounded great. After the phone call, I got out an encyclopedia and learned that she was referring to Rio de Janeiro. In Brazil. Where they speak Portuguese. I had a little Spanish in high school, but I didn't know any Portuguese.

Fortunately, I was placed with a wonderful Brazilian family, and they all spoke English. They seemed thrilled to have me stay with them. I had a younger brother, an older college-age brother, and two sisters close to my age. It was an incredible experience, and I wouldn't trade those five months for anything.

I learned so much from my Brazilian sisters, Maria Regina and Angela. Both were experienced seamstresses, and they taught me to design my clothes and make my own patterns. They also taught me to "make a touca" which is a method of straightening hair by winding it around the head and securing it with bobby pins. Until then, the only way I knew of to straighten my naturally curly/wavy hair was by ironing it. Ironing hair was popular in the 1960s, before curling irons and straight irons, but not an ideal way to get sleek healthy hair. Some girls set their hair on beer cans to smooth out the curls, but that was too uncomfortable.

Maria Regina, me, and Angela in Rio in 1968.

In Rio, we lived in a nice, spacious apartment on an upper floor. There were several embassies on our street, Rua das Laranjeiras, including the British Embassy. One day, I watched from a window as Queen Elizabeth and Prince Philip went by in a large black car with the top down, waving at crowds gathered along the street.

I was excited when my Brazilian family took me to see legendary soccer star, Pelé, play in the famed Maracanã Stadium. I knew nothing about soccer, but I understood it was a once-in-a-lifetime experience for this American girl.

While I was in Brazil, Mom hosted an Argentine student named Patricio. He lived with Mom and Mike for six months. Although it may have strained the budget some, I'm sure Mom felt that since another family was hosting me, she wanted to return the favor. She didn't like to be obligated to anyone. Patricio was delightful, handsome, and polite. My mom and Mike thoroughly enjoyed having him in our home. He was still with my family after I came back from Brazil, so I got to know him, too. I have lost touch with Patricio, but I think he's in Paris working for the Argentine government.

My Brazilian family: Angela, Luis Felipe, Maria Regina, Virginie and Robert. Sergio, the older brother, isn't in the picture.

I kept in touch with my Brazilian family through letters, photos, and rare phone calls after returning home. Twenty-eight years later, Mariana, the daughter of my older Brazilian brother, Sergio, came to stay with our family, further strengthening the bond between the two families.

In 1997, Steve, Mom, and I went to Brazil for a week-long stay. It was like no time had passed at all since I'd been there the first time in 1968. My Brazilian family was excited to see me, and they were so happy to meet Mom and Steve. We stayed in their home, and they treated us like royalty. They showed us all the sites that they had taken me to when I was there the first time but were new to Steve and Mom: Sugarloaf Mountain, Ipanema and Copacabana beaches, and the magnificent 98-foot tall statue Christ the Redeemer at the summit of Mount Corcovado. The statue was pictured on the cover of one of my geography books when I was in high school, so it was almost surreal on my first trip to see it with my own eyes. Steve and Mom were equally impressed.

Mom and Mariana on Leblon Beach in front of
Sugarloaf Mountain in Rio de Janeiro during our visit in 1997.

We flew home on standby tickets, courtesy of my brother, Mike, who worked for American Airlines. We had a change of planes in São Paulo, and when we arrived at the airport, we discovered our flight to Miami had been canceled. We were concerned we might have to spend the night in the São Paulo airport; or worse, that it would close at midnight and we'd have to find a place to sleep in the huge city. None of us spoke much Portuguese, further complicating our situation.

We were all anxious, but Mom was beside herself, telling Steve and me we should be trying harder to get on a plane. Her anxiety only increased my anxiety, and I finally told her angrily, "We're all worried about staying overnight at this airport, but we've talked to the desk agents and there's nothing we can do but wait and see. You getting so upset only makes me more upset and is not at all helpful!"

It was probably the only time in my life I raised my voice in anger to her. Mom backed off, and I know she was hurt, but I didn't apologize. Not until later, anyway.

We were in the São Paulo airport for about six hours when it was announced there was a flight leaving for Dallas/Ft. Worth in a few minutes. We knew we could get a flight home to Iowa from Dallas, American Airlines' hub, so we signed up for standby seats. We were afraid the passengers who had been booked on the canceled Miami flight would fill up the Dallas flight, and there wouldn't be room for us.

A long line of people boarded, and when it appeared the plane was about to leave without us, the agent called our names. When we got to the desk, he pointed to the door going outside, and said one word to us: "Run!" We ran through the door, across the tarmac, and up a flight of portable steps to the plane. There were plenty of seats, and we breathed a sigh of relief. The rest of the seven-hour trip went smoothly. Only when we arrived safely on U.S. soil did I speak to Mom again.

I felt bad about "yelling" at her. I'm not sure I ever learned the best way to deal with her disapproval. I couldn't seem to let her criticism roll off my back as Susan and Mike did. Instead, I internalized it. Mom had told me many years before that when I was mad at her as a toddler, I'd pick leaves off her house plants when I thought she wasn't looking. As an adult, I usually just held my tongue.

13
Leaving Home

When I went off to college, I felt a sense of freedom I had never known while living at home. I think Susan felt the same way, but she wasn't as sensitive to Mom's mood swings as I was. Mike had two years left of high school, but by the time he was a teenager, he and Mom had a comfortable relationship. Like Susan, he wasn't as bothered by her moods and criticism as I was.

I decided to attend a small Christian college in Nebraska. My primary reason for the choice was that my first serious boyfriend was attending that college. I started dating him when I was a high school freshman and he was a senior. By the time I graduated from high school, he'd moved on to greener pastures, but I decided to enroll there anyway. I'd visited the school several times, and it seemed like a good fit for me – boyfriend or no boyfriend. When people ask me how long our relationship lasted, I wryly tell them I dated him for three years and he dated me for one. That's an exaggeration. I dated other guys in high school, but usually only once or twice. That's all the time it took for me to decide they weren't what I was looking for.

Susan transferred from a state college after her

freshman year to the college I planned to attend. She was dating my former boyfriend's brother who was also enrolled there. Mom wasn't happy we were going to a church school that wasn't accredited. She thought we were just following our boyfriends (and the potential to meet new boyfriends) without any thought to career goals, which was mostly true.

My choice of colleges turned out to be a good one for several reasons, but especially because that's where I met my future husband, Steve. Although shy and quiet, he worked up the courage to ask me to go with him to Wednesday night chapel for our first date. I wasn't all that interested in this bashful red-haired farm boy from Iowa until we stood to sing. That's when I heard this beautiful voice and realized it was coming from him. Steve may have been lacking in confidence when it came to girls, but he sang with the self-assurance and talent of a professional.

Mom and Steve in 1987.

I joke that "I married Steve for his singing voice – his voice and his money – but it turned out he didn't have any money, so it was really just the voice thing." Of course, there were other, more significant reasons. I married him because he is the kindest, most loving, and most patient person I've ever met. But it was the way he sang that first hooked me. My mom, for once, totally approved of my choice. I used to tease her, saying she liked him better than me. We were engaged exactly one year after our first date.

As much as Mom liked Steve, she thought we were too young to get married – we were a couple of months away from being 20. She finally came around, probably because she thought so highly of Steve. His dad had to sign for him to get a marriage license because at that time men had to be 21 to get married in Wisconsin. I didn't need a parent's signature because women only had to be 18.

We were married at the Readstown church I grew up in on May 29, 1971. In my father's absence, Mike rang the church bell seven times at 7 p.m. and then walked me down the aisle. Steve sang "Walk Hand in Hand with Me" as we held hands and faced each other. We exchanged silver bands, engraved inside with the title of a song by the Carpenters, "We've Only Just Begun." The song was sung at our wedding by a friend.

I got the idea of engraving our rings from one of my favorite books. It's the story of Mary Todd and Abraham Lincoln, whose wedding rings were engraved with the words "Love is Eternal," which is also the title of the book. The Lincolns' inscription was, perhaps, a little weightier than words from a pop song, but at the age of not-quite 20, it was meaningful to us.

Mom made my wedding dress, and it was pretty, but it wasn't the dress I had imagined and designed myself. She changed the design because she thought it would improve the look of the dress. Although I wanted the exact dress I'd drawn for her, I didn't have the courage or stamina to fight for it.

My wedding was a blur – literally. I wore hard contacts, but they hurt my eyes after just a few hours. I didn't want to have red eyes throughout my wedding and reception, so I planned to wait until just before the ceremony to put in the contacts. In the rush, I forgot and went to my wedding without contacts or glasses. As a kid, I often forgot to wear my glasses to school. My mom worked out of town, so she couldn't deliver them to me like other kids' mothers. She used to tell me, only half-jokingly, "Mary, I hope you never have kids, or you'll leave them somewhere!" I am happy to say I never forgot my kids and never left them anywhere. Not once!

Steve and I walk down the aisle after our wedding ceremony in 1971.

After we were married, before the guests were dismissed, the pastor rushed us to the church basement to sign the marriage license. After we signed it, he looked at our signatures and pointed out that I had signed "the wrong name." I had signed "Mary McSwain." I had to squeeze in "Steele." Inadvertently, I had kept my maiden name, before it was fashionable for women to do so.

That was 49 years ago, and we are still together – by choice, not because of the piece of paper we signed. I promised myself when I was in my early teens that I would never get a divorce because I knew first-hand how hard divorce is on children. When Steve and I started dating, I dreaded telling him that my parents were divorced. He was raised in a very conservative home and a church where divorce wasn't acceptable. I thought if he knew, he might not want to date me. I was greatly relieved when he said it didn't matter, and it wouldn't affect our relationship.

Steve tells me he loves me every day, to which I sometimes respond (for variety): "Of course you do! How could you not?" He also tells me daily I'm beautiful. Often my reply is, "We've got to get you in to see my optometrist!" I guess it's no secret who the romantic is in this relationship.

Despite my sometimes flippant responses, Steve knows I love him and that I think he's beautiful – inside and out. We can't imagine life without the other one, although there will come a time when, almost certainly, one of us will experience being left alone. We have a wall hanging that reads: "When we have each other, we have everything." A cliché, but true. Steve is my rock. My anchor. Without him, I don't know how I would have gotten through my mom's illness and death, which is the most painful experience I've had in my 69 years.

14
Kind Words

Day 13: December 24, 2008

I was getting ready to go to the hospital one morning just before Christmas when it occurred to me that we could create a nursing scholarship in Mom's name at Iowa Lakes Community College. After retiring and moving to Spencer, Mom worked part-time as a proctor for TV classes at Iowa Lakes, which is also where I was the director of a volunteer program. I shared the scholarship idea with Mom as soon as I got to the hospital. She loved it.

We talked about the qualifications and guidelines. Mom wanted the scholarship to go to a nursing student who had experience as a nurse aide. The nurse aides had been a great blessing to us all in the days she'd been hospitalized. Mom was okay with the recipient not being the best student in the class. She said her grades were average when she was in nurses' training. She also wanted the scholarship to be awarded to a student who, without a scholarship, might struggle financially. In other words, she wanted it to go to someone like herself.

The Elizabeth McSwain Nursing Scholarship would

be for $1,000 for three years, with the option of extending it into future years. She was clearly pleased with this small legacy she was leaving, and the time passed quickly as we worked out the details.

Because Mom was always a very private person, it was no surprise that she didn't want visitors to see her so ill. She allowed only two friends, Maxine and Donna, to visit. Later, her grandchildren and great-grandchildren would come from out of town to say goodbye, but otherwise, it was just Susan and her husband, Dennis, Steve, and me with her during her hospitalization.

Most people would think being at the hospital over the holidays would be especially depressing, but in some ways, it was a blessing. Because the college is closed between Christmas and New Year's, I didn't have to worry so much about missing work. I sent an email to my supervisor explaining my situation and he replied, "Don't worry about it. Do what you need to do." I was greatly relieved by his empathetic response. I stayed in touch with my office staff using my laptop, as did Susan, who was a social worker.

A special event occurred on Christmas Eve after I'd gone home at the end of another seemingly endless day. Susan and Mom had heard singing in the halls. A group of carolers came into Mom's room singing Christmas carols. Their songs cheered Mom and Susan and brought tears to their eyes. Before leaving, the carolers gave Mom a red fleece blanket with Ho-Ho-Ho printed on it. We put the blanket on top of her bedspread, and it gave the sterile hospital room a warm holiday touch. I wish I could tell the singers what a difference they made to all of us and thank them for giving up their time on Christmas Eve to cheer patients and families, but I never learned who they were. They may have been part of a church group or perhaps some of the hospital staff.

Cousins Nancy, Annette, Gene, and their spouses sent a beautiful Christmas floral arrangement, and Mom's good friend, Bonnie, sent flowers. Bonnie lived 100 miles away and was too frail to visit, but Mom called her to say goodbye. There were plants, flowers, and cards from other friends as well.

Our grandkids, who ranged in age from seven months to eight years, made cards for Great-Grandma Betty which we taped to the wall where she could see them from her hospital bed. The messages from the great-grandchildren included sweet and thoughtful advice such as: "Get better," and "It's okay to be sad," as well as loving notes saying "U r the best grrdma" and "I luv you, Grandma."

Mom's friends, many who lived in her condo complex, sent cards with truly heartfelt messages:

...You will be in my thoughts during the times ahead. I want to tell you that you were one of the most accepting and concerned folks in the building. We appreciate that. Thank you again for telling me I was a faithful caregiver to Ray (her husband). *I do hope you will have faithful caregivers in this difficult time. God be with you.*

And this one:

I am so sorry to hear about your illness. You have been a good and helpful neighbor. It has been a pleasure knowing you... Betty, hang in there and know everyone is praying for you. May God bless you and keep you in his care. I loved your rice pudding...

I always smile when I read the last line. And I'm sure my Mom liked hearing her friend say she loved her rice pudding.

Another friend remembered Mom's adventurous spirit:

I am so sad to know you are ill. I can't believe it — I have never been so shocked... I want you to know how much knowing you has meant to me. I think you are the bravest person I have ever known with all you did in your professional life. I loved hearing about your adventures with a lot of envy. I will always remember you with fondness and gratitude.

This note came from the director of People 4 Pets, a non-profit, no-kill animal shelter in Spencer where Mom loved working as a volunteer:

> *... I think of you often, Betty, and pray for you. We miss your sweet smile and kind words of encouragement at People 4 Pets. Thank you so much for your special love of all the animals.*

These friends of Mom's, many of whom were in their eighties when they wrote the notes, put me to shame. When – *if* – I get around to sending a get-well or sympathy card, I usually write some overused but well-intended phrase like, "You're in my thoughts and prayers." The notes sent to my mom are heartfelt and powerful. I keep the cards to remind me how just a few kind words can make a difference. Besides giving me comfort, their notes revealed to me a side of my mom that I didn't always see for myself.

Mom was genuinely surprised that so many people sent cards and gifts, and she was touched by the sincere, thoughtful messages they wrote. At first, Mom read every card herself. After a few days, as she got weaker, she asked us to read them to her. I couldn't read a card aloud without choking up. Every time I started reading something nice that someone had written, I would have to hand the card to Susan to finish reading it.

Mom was amused and a little annoyed – she was never a crier herself. I felt useless and ridiculous at being unable to control my emotions, especially in Mom's presence. She needed us to be strong, and I was often finding it difficult to hold it together. Fortunately, Susan and Mom were more emotionally stable throughout the experience.

15
Grandma Betty

Since Mom had found our poems entertaining when we were younger, it seemed fitting that I would use poetry to announce the upcoming arrival of our first child, her first grandchild. I sent the poem to Mom, postmarked December 19, 1972, with a note on the back of the envelope in red marker: "To be opened on Christmas Day!"

> *You said you didn't want*
> *A Christmas present this year.*
> *And so we've something better*
> *To fill your day with cheer.*
> *It didn't cost a penny*
> *(I hope you don't think we're cheap)*
> *But it's something we think you'll want,*
> *And something we know you'll keep.*
>
> *And if by now you haven't guessed,*
> *We'll give you a little clue —*
> *A stork will bring it, not Santa,*
> *All wrapped in pink or blue.*
> *But you have to keep it a secret*

For nobody else must know
Until we tell Susan, Mike, and Grams
That our family's going to grow.

This gift will be a little late.
Of course, you'll understand why
But we hope you'll have a Merry Christmas
On the 15th of July!

Love and Kisses,
Steve and Mary

True to our word, Joseph Steven was born July 15, 1973, a week after his due date. I picked the 15th for the poem because my sisters-in-law said first babies were always late. Mom and Grandma Rosson came to Nebraska, where we were living and going to college, to meet Joey.

His eyes were very blue, like my mom's. My eyes are brown, and Steve's are hazel. After Grandma and Mom returned to Wisconsin and Steve went back to work, I was alone with the baby for the first time. He cried all day and didn't sleep. Steve came home from work to a wife and son both in tears. Within minutes, he had gotten Joey to go to sleep, tucking the baby under his arm in the traditional football hold, walking and singing. I got a much-needed break.

A few weeks after Joey's birth, we visited Mom in Wisconsin. She had purchased a pretty 100-year-old rocker so she could rock Joey and future grandchildren. She would have four more grandchildren over the next few years. One of my favorite pictures is of her, soon after getting home from work and still in her nurse's uniform, holding Joey in the rocker.

Our second child, Aaron Michael, was born in 1975, and Laura Ellyn arrived in 1977. We are blessed with caring, intelligent, insightful, and witty kids. They are the lights of our lives. When they tell us how lucky we are to have such

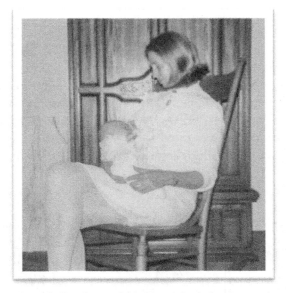

*Mom holding Joey in the rocking chair she bought to rock
her first grandchild and all of her future grandchildren.*

good kids, we tell them glibly it was our exceptional parenting
that made them the good people they are. To be honest, the
way they turned out probably has less to do with our
parenting and more to do with their ability to make good
choices. But ultimately, they are who they are because of
God's love and grace.

I gained a new appreciation for my mom and other
single moms after we had children. That's when I began to
realize what a huge responsibility it must have been for Mom
to raise three children by herself on a very limited budget. I
have a loving and helpful husband, our income was adequate,
and still, there were times when we both felt at the end of our
ropes after a particularly trying day. Mom could be
unreasonable, impatient, and demanding. I understood her
better when I became a parent.

I used to think this quote said everything about
raising children: "The best thing a father can do for his

children is to love their mother." Although I still think it's critical to the well-being of the children, I've learned that it's not enough. A father also needs to be there for his family, not only physically, but emotionally and spiritually as well. Steve understands that and lives it as a husband and parent.

Our children made excellent choices in choosing their mates. Joe married Nicole Kathleen, Aaron married Nicole Maria, and Laura married David. Our kids have given us the best gifts we could ever hope for – 10 happy, creative grandchildren who bring us more joy than we ever imagined.

Our children and grandchildren: (Front Row) Timothy, Benjamin, Anna, Jack (Row 2) Charlie, Allison, Trevor, Caleb, Rowan, Sam (Row 3) Nicole Kathleen, Laura, me, Nicole Maria, (Back Row) Joe, Dave, Steve, Aaron

Our grandchildren, her great-grandchildren, were all under eight years old when Mom died. It saddens me to think they won't remember much, if anything, about her. I am glad they will have this book to read someday so they can get to know Great-Grandma Betty.

Mom meets her 14th great-grandchild, Caleb, born to Laura and Dave in May 2008, eight months before she died. Mom didn't get to meet her 15th great-grandchild, Riley McKenzie Thompson, who was born to my brother's daughter Leslie (McSwain) and Steve Thompson in August 2014.

16
Michael Rosson McSwain

Mom was terrified of storms, and in particular, tornadoes, which occasionally ripped through Southwest Wisconsin. When Susan, Mike, and I were young, and there was lightning all around followed closely by loud claps of thunder, Mom would say to us, "Rain makes the flowers grow." She thought it would reassure us, but it was Mom who needed reassurance. I grew up not being afraid of storms, as did my sister and brother.

Me (4), Mike (2), and Susan (5) in 1955.

Mom's biggest worry when we were young centered on Mike. She was concerned about her son being raised by a single mother. When Mike displayed effeminate qualities as a very young child, she was visibly upset. Mom tried to get him to change some of his behaviors: how he walked, his hand motions, the way he spoke with a slight lisp. It bothered her, and she thought he exhibited those tendencies because there wasn't "a man in the house" as a role model. She signed him up for Boy Scouts and Little League Baseball.

Mike, 1956

Mike married Jan, a social worker, in March 1976. They had a daughter, Leslie, born in August 1977. She was Mike's pride and joy. We didn't see them often because we were in Iowa, and Mike and Jan lived in Florida. Their marriage didn't last long. They divorced in September 1978.

I was in my 30s when I began to realize Mike was gay. We visited him in Mobile, Alabama, where he moved after his divorce. Mike and his male roommate were the perfect hosts. It wasn't until after we spent several days there it occurred to me that he might be gay. Looking back, it's hard to believe how naïve I was. He and his roommate shared the master bedroom, and their relationship seemed more like a comfortably married couple than good friends. I guess I thought they were sharing the master to accommodate overnight guests while we were there.

At that time, I didn't know anyone who was gay, or, to be more accurate, I wasn't aware of anyone who I knew was gay. I asked Susan what she thought, and she confirmed he was. Mike and I didn't talk about his sexual orientation until almost 10 years later, and then not face to face, but through an exchange of letters. Mike sent a letter to Mom, Susan, and me, dated December 29, 1996, when he was 43, in which he wrote about being gay. These are excerpts from the four-page, single-spaced, typed letter he wrote to us:

...I do thank you, my family, for being as supportive as you can. To one of you, or maybe two of you, I know that my lifestyle has been an embarrassment to you. I will say this, and I know it's something you have heard before, but never from me: Being gay is who I am, it is not something I chose to be. And unless you are gay yourself, you really cannot know the feeling of simply 'being gay.' Someday, science will prove the theories supporting this. It has nothing to do with the way I was raised. It is just there. If it isn't 'just there,' please explain why at 10 years old or so, I had a strong attraction to males...

...The point I am trying to make here is this: Just like inheriting green eyes and blonde hair, so, too, is the gene that controls sexual orientation. Trust me on this. If anyone, whether it be friends or family members, lead a gay lifestyle or have real problems dealing with the straight world, please, please, give them latitude and understanding. There are too many suicides of young people who are gay, whose parents do not accept them the way they are. They take their lives because they

know they can never live up to the expectations of their families...

Mike closes with this:

...I know I may sound like a martyr — I really don't want to be that. But I cannot keep these feelings in anymore. I love every one of you.

Love, Michael

It's interesting — and heart-breaking — that although Mike had come out and confirmed his gay lifestyle, he still felt the need to apologize to his family. I'm sure he thought we'd be offended by his being openly gay.

I responded to Mike with an equally long letter. I knew his reference to one of his family members being embarrassed by his lifestyle was directed at me. I reminded him he had never told me he was gay, and that I didn't figure it out for sure until Susan told me.

I continued the letter by saying, "I have always believed that people were gay because they were born that way. I don't believe that people choose the lifestyle because they like being different. And, by the way, I don't believe that AIDS is God's punishment for people who are gay," which was the popular opinion expressed by some conservative Christians in the 1980s and '90s (and probably still today). I closed by assuring him I loved him regardless of his sexual orientation.

I thought I truly believed all that I told Mike in my letter. But I've been thinking recently that if I really meant it, if I wasn't embarrassed by his sexual orientation, why didn't I tell people he was gay? It has been only in the last few years that I started to tell close friends I had a brother who was gay. What finally prompted me to share my family secret with friends and acquaintances was that I got tired of hearing them tell jokes about people who are gay, or worse, being judgmental about alternative lifestyles. Mentioning that my brother was gay usually silenced them, at least when I was within earshot.

I think when you know and care about someone who is gay, it's less difficult to accept their lifestyle and love them anyway. If you are not close to anyone who is gay, it's easier to be judgmental. I am reminded of a quote in "Bird by Bird," by Ann Lamott, which she attributes to her friend Father Tom: "You can safely assume you've created God in your own image when it turns out that God hates all the same people you do."

Mike matured into a tall, handsome blonde, and my mom enjoyed being in his company. They often traveled together, and she even lived with him and his partner in Mobile for a while. She accepted him the way he was, although it may have taken her a while. According to Mike's letter, she was still trying to fix him up with young women a few years before he wrote it. I'm not sure when her attitude changed – perhaps when she met his partner and liked him. She loved her only son, her youngest child, and she wanted him in her life.

Mom and her friend Bonnie in New Orleans
with Mike and his daughter, Leslie.

When Mike came to our house in Spencer for a visit just before Christmas in 1994, I distinctly remember thinking he looked too thin. We hadn't seen him for a while. He had moved from Mobile to Arlington, Texas, and didn't always make it home for holidays. As soon as he put away his luggage, Mike told Susan, Mom, and me what we instinctively knew – he was sick. He told us he had AIDS.

He said he probably contracted the disease in the late 1970s before most people knew what AIDS was. Mike attempted to soften the blow by saying some treatments would slow the progress of the disease. Mom tried to appear stoic, but we knew her heart was breaking. Susan and I thought she was hearing the news for the first time as we were. As it turns out, he had told her the devastating news in a letter written two weeks earlier. I didn't find the letter until after Mom died in 2009. The handwritten eight-page letter was dated November 14, 1994:

I guess it's time to sit down and write this letter. I cannot put it off much longer. If you're not sitting down, you may want to sit down for this one.

Six weeks ago, I went to the doctor. I thought I had just screwed up my body with my diet. I had a complete physical including the AIDS test. A week later, I got the news the AIDS test was positive. I went in the next day to get some blood work done for my T-cell count, the cells that fight the infection. Normal counts are 700-1700. Mine was 87. The doctor then referred me to an infectious disease specialist where I was given a lot of information about where I am and where I'm going. The doctor estimated I was infected 12 to 15 years ago. I asked the doctor how long I had. He first said, 'years,' and then changed it to 'a couple of years...'

Mike went on to tell about the medications he was taking and the treatments he would undergo to keep the disease in check. He said he'd spent several weeks getting "paperwork in order," including his will. He closed the letter with some comments about his frame of mind.

I realize it is going to be difficult and probably depressing when we get together at Thanksgiving, but I want us to celebrate life. I am alive — I have beaten the odds of living the usual 5-7 years with AIDS. Unfortunately, I know I am fighting a battle that I cannot win. But I can give it a run for the money!

If I seem a bit too positive about this, it is because I have had three weeks to think about it. I have, I think, made my peace with God, and I thank Him daily for each day He gives me.

I am sorry to have to tell you this. I wish it could have been more pleasant news. Don't be angry with me — I'm sorry. I love you.

Michael

On the front of the envelope, Mike wrote a message to Mom she would read before opening his letter: "At least I'm not asking for money this time!"

Like keeping it a secret that my brother was gay, I didn't tell anyone that he had AIDS. I told them he was undergoing chemo treatment (which was true), and they automatically thought he had cancer. Mike remained relatively healthy for six years, but in December 2000, we knew his condition was deteriorating rapidly. He decided to discontinue chemotherapy. Mom and Susan flew from Iowa to Texas to help with his care for the last couple of weeks. Steve and I had gone to see Mike at Thanksgiving. It had been a depressing visit, and I hadn't planned to be with him when he died.

But in mid-January, Susan and Mom called and asked me to come. Although Mike was too weak to speak, they said he would often hold up four fingers, which was an effort for him. They couldn't understand what he was trying to tell them. Finally, Susan asked him, "Mary?" and he relaxed. Susan thinks he was saying he wanted the four of us — Mom, Susan, Leslie, and me — there together and no visitors except his best friend and former partner, Greg. Mike and Greg had traveled extensively together, and he helped care for Mike while he was sick. Steve and I packed quickly and made the

Mike with Mom and Leslie in 1989.

13-hour trip to Arlington, Texas, stopping only for gas.

When we arrived at Mike's home, I was shocked and deeply disturbed at how emaciated he was. The images of him in bed would haunt me for a long time afterward. He was in a semi-conscious state, heavily sedated with painkillers. He was unable to see well due to detached retinas caused by the disease. Even so, it was clear Mike knew I was there when I walked into his room and spoke to him. When he heard my voice, his eyes opened, and he tilted his head to hear me. Over the next few days, I would often go to his bedside, tell him I loved him, and tell him it was okay to leave us.

On Jan. 19, 2001, we were in Mike's living room when Leslie heard a sound coming from his bedroom. She jumped up and went into his room, the rest of us following her. We watched as he took his final breaths. Mom would later say she saw a vapor – a spirit? – rise above his body after he stopped breathing. I think that gave her great comfort. He was 47 years old.

Michael Rosson McSwain, 1953-2001

17
Happy Trails

Day 16: December 27, 2008

The Saturday after Christmas our kids came home to celebrate the holidays with us and to visit Grandma Betty at the hospital. Although we didn't know how much time Mom had left, they all understood this would be their last chance to see her and talk to her. Susan and I combed her hair, and she put in her false teeth with great difficulty. She hadn't worn them after the first few days in the hospital, and it was hard for her to get them in, but she managed. I was relieved she was able to wear the dentures. She looked frail and sick with her teeth, but without them, she was barely recognizable. It would be the last time she would be able to make the effort.

I always felt bad about Mom's teeth. She would often comment on someone's "nice smile" or "white teeth" before she mentioned their eyes, hair, or skin. I don't think her parents took her to a dentist as a child because of the cost, and fluoride wasn't added to the water supply like it was when I was a child. Even though she took very good care of her teeth as an adult, she had several pulled over the years and replaced by partials. Finally, she'd lost so many that the dentist said she needed to have them all pulled and replaced with dentures. She was home from traveling for a brief time, so she had to have the work done all in one day. Mom said she was in the dentist's chair for hours, and it was an awful, exhausting experience. Even though money was tight when we were growing up, Mom always made sure her children went to the dentist regularly.

When Joe and Nicole arrived at the hospital, we took a few pictures of Mom with their kids and with the flower arrangements sent by friends and family. They are the last photos taken of Mom. In the pictures, you can tell she's enduring the photo session rather than enjoying it. Even in healthier, happier times, she disliked having her picture taken. In many of the family snapshots, she is holding her hand out in front of her face, blocking the camera lens.

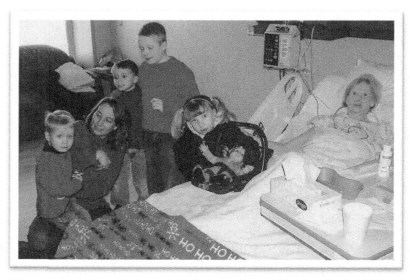

Our kids and grandkids came to say goodbye at the hospital. Joe took this last picture we have of Mom (with Nicole and their children, Trevor, Charlie, Tim, and Allison).

Aaron, Nicole, Laura, and Dave, along with their children, came to visit that afternoon. It was a bittersweet time. We knew Mom wasn't feeling well, and she wasn't used to having so many people in her room all at once. After the great-grandkids visited briefly with her, Steve took them to the waiting room at the end of the hall so our children could spend time with their grandma. When our daughter, Laura, and her family left the hospital room, she hugged Mom and said goodbye. Mom replied, "I'll just say 'Happy Trails.'" She couldn't bring herself to say "goodbye."

A few days later, with our encouragement, Mom called Leslie, Mike's daughter, and Jill, Susan's daughter, to tell them goodbye. It was difficult for Mom and her granddaughters to say goodbye over the phone, but Iowa's January weather and their distance from Spencer made it difficult for them to visit Grandma Betty at the hospital.

18
Seeing the World

After her children graduated from high school and left home, Mom began looking for opportunities to travel. She had always wanted to see the world, so when she noticed an ad in a medical journal advertising for nurses to work in Saudi Arabia, she applied. The King Faisal Specialist Hospital in the capital city of Riyadh was new, large, and modern. No expense was spared on the hospital where the King and his family would receive specialized medical treatment along with Saudi citizens and foreigners. Nurses from all over the world were needed to care for patients since Saudi women were not allowed to work outside the home. Mom was hired and left for Riyadh in January 1975 when she 50.

Although I knew this was a great opportunity for her, I was disappointed that she was leaving a few months before our second son, Aaron, was born. She would not find out about the birth of her grandson until our letter arrived almost two weeks later. Mom was still in Saudi Arabia when Mike's daughter, Leslie, was born, and when our daughter, Laura, arrived two years after Aaron. Mom wrote to congratulate us a week after Laura's birth:

Congratulations! And to think it was a girl, too! You chose a pretty name. The Telex arrived on June 28th. The only problem was that it was signed Harry and Steve! Who is this Harry that Steve lives with? Glad you're all okay… How do Joey and Aaron like the wee one? Does she have red hair – blue or brown eyes? Now it's time for you to quit – take the advice of one who knows – or tell me to mind my own business.

I still smile when I read that. It is so like my mom to offer advice on how many children we should have.

We were concerned for Mom's safety, being a single American woman in a middle-eastern country. She pointed out that she could "get hit by a truck while crossing the street" in Readstown. Looking back, I am amazed she didn't seem anxious about traveling to and living in a foreign country compared to a small, almost crime-free, midwestern town. I think it shows how determined she was to finally leave Readstown and see all the places she'd only read about.

Three months after Mom arrived in Riyadh, King Faisal, 68, was shot point-blank and killed by his half-brother's son, Prince Faisal, who had a history of mental illness. Prince Faisal was executed – beheaded in the city square. The throne went to King Faisal's son, Crown Prince Khalid. Because of Khalid's poor health, the actual ruling of the Saudi kingdom was handled by King Faisal's half-brother, Fahd.

Mom expressed concern about retribution as a result of the King's assassination and the possibility of an uprising, but things remained relatively calm. Shortly after King Faisal's death, Mom was asked to join the circle of mourners at the palace, which was large and beautiful, and "there was gold everywhere," she said. The mourners sat in a circle with King Faisal's widow, and no one spoke. After a set amount of time, Mom said, "We rose from our chairs and quietly left the palace."

There were many restrictions on women's dress and behavior in the 1970s which were strictly enforced, and many still exist today in Saudi Arabia. The restrictions applied to women from the U.S. as well as other countries when they were out in public. Mom had to cover her head with a scarf, wear long sleeves or a shawl, and hide her legs with a long skirt or pants when she went sightseeing or to the grocery store. The restrictions didn't apply when she was at the hospital where she always wore her nurse's uniform or when she was in the compound where the foreign employees lived.

Saudi Arabia had, and still has, extremely harsh punishment for crimes. Judges had total power over sentencing because there was no legal code and no way for convicted criminals to appeal. Alcohol is not allowed in Saudi, and anyone caught drinking would be jailed for several days. A foreigner accused of drinking would be thrown out of the country after serving jail time. Thieves caught in the act of stealing were taken to the city square where an executioner would chop off the offending hand. Crimes like murder, rape, witchcraft, adultery, and speaking against the government would likely result in public stoning, lashing, or beheading. Large crowds gathered to watch the public executions. After making the mistake of accidentally walking by the square and witnessing one, Mom and her friends avoided the area when executions were scheduled.

A young Saudi man named Kashmir served as a tour guide on several trips for a group of nurses that included my mom. They were fond of him and enjoyed his company, and they were horrified to find out that Kashmir had been executed. The nurses never found out what his crime was. Mom said they worried for a long time that the authorities would come looking for them since they'd spent a lot of time with Kashmir, but the nurses were never contacted.

Because the threat of extreme punishment deterred most criminal activity, Mom felt safe in Saudi. She said women could leave their purses at the front of a grocery store while shopping and the purses would be there, untouched, when they were done shopping. Despite her feelings of security, Mom was pickpocketed at the airport in Riyadh, which is considered to be one of the safest, most crime-free places in the world. She was always careful to hold on tightly to her purse which had a shoulder strap she wore across her chest. She was shocked that the pickpocket was able to get into her purse and take all the bills out of her checkbook, around which she had tightly stretched a rubber band. After expertly removing the cash, the thief returned the checkbook to her purse with the rubber band untouched. My mom had no idea she was being robbed, but she does remember someone bumping against her shoulder while standing in line at the airport check-in desk.

Mom and Saudi guide, Kashmir, in the Himalayas. He was later executed for reasons unknown to Mom and the other nurses.

We received letters from Mom on a semi-regular basis, as the mail from Saudi wasn't always dependable. It's possible her letters were inspected before being sent on to the U.S. In one of her first letters, written a few weeks after arriving in Riyadh, she updated us on her adjustment to her new surroundings.

I'm settling in O.K. My social life is nil, but when we work nine hours a day, I'm too tired to go out at night anyway. Well, that's the plight of us old ladies… So far, I like it. It's really different from what I expected from reading all those books. The weather is cool – the sun shines all day. We had a dust storm Friday… The hospital isn't completed yet, but when it is, it really will be the greatest hospital in the world. It is so automated and computerized, you wouldn't believe it.

Mom goes on to describe in detail all the technology built into the hospital, which was ahead of its time in 1975. She adds, "This is really a beautiful hospital, and to say it cost 100 million dollars is a very low estimate, I'm sure." She continues:

Went on a tour of the King Faisal Conference Hall where Saudi and Gulf States hold their government conferences. It was really beautiful. Then another nurse and I went to a Nina Ricci showing of clothes, most of which were priced at $1,400 to $1,500. Not bad for a little hunk of material. Guess I'll stick with JCPenney.
One of my housemates got sent home after spending 48 hours in jail – supposedly for drinking and dating a Saudi… One of our pharmacists is in the Riyadh jail for poking a Saudi in the face because the Saudi had parked his car so the pharmacist couldn't move his. The dumb nut (pharmacist) should have known better. We're warned of those things. He's been in jail a week. As soon as the hospital can get him released, they'll have to get him out of the country.
The political situation in this part of the country doesn't look too good. Wonder when it will all blow up… Many of the hospital employees, especially single females, are leaving because of the restrictions on us. Now we have to show our IDs if we come in after midnight. And,

of course, men are not allowed in our quarters, nor us in theirs.

Whenever we (women) go to class or work anywhere outside our dorm, we have to walk with at least one other person. We distract the workers so. It's just like a circus. They all lay down their shovels or stop whatever they're doing and look at us. These aren't American or English, but the Arabs (from countries outside of Saudi like Yemen, Palestine, etc.). As it is explained to me, these fellows have probably never seen a woman unveiled except their mothers and sisters.

Yesterday, a group of 40 or more women came through the hospital to look it over. One was a royal group from Mali (Western Africa). I believe one of them was the Queen of Mali, but I'm not sure. The women had soldiers with them to protect them.

Mom wrote a few months later that they'd had other distinguished guests come for the ribbon cutting at the new hospital:

Well, this past week has been another biggie. We entertained no less than Anwar Sadat, president of Egypt, King Khaled of Saudi Arabia, and Crown Prince Fahd of Saudi Arabia. Of course, their whole entourage was with them. I am sending you each a piece of the ribbon cut by President Sadat and King Khaled. They arrived with sirens blowing, police cars, and then the Royal Palace Guards in ten bright red cars with the tops down, five or six soldiers in each car. The soldiers wore khaki-colored uniforms with red berets and carried machine guns, bayonets, and rifles... The King, Crown Prince, and President Sadat followed in three big black Rolls Royces. The night before, Anwar Sadat's personal physician along with other dignitaries came through our clinic. At his request, I checked his reflexes and a few other things. They were a friendly bunch of fellows...

After the King had been in our department, one of the Palace Guards wanted his blood pressure checked, so I took it. Then they all — about 15 of them — wanted their BP taken. They came into my room throwing machine guns left and right. None of them spoke English, but I'd show them the numbers and then I'd say, 'quais' which means 'good,' and they'd laugh and shake hands.

I looked up the Arabic word *quais* and it means, "I'm

well" instead of "you're well" or "good." Maybe that's why they laughed. Mom may have told the Royal Palace Guards that *she* was well instead of what she meant: *Your* blood pressure is good.

On another occasion, a bunch of high-ranking military men came through. Prince Bandar was with the group — he is King Faisal's son and the best-looking guy ever, especially in his General's uniform... We're hearing that the Shah of Iran is coming next week.

I had never heard of Prince Bandar, and I thought Mom's comment about him being the "the best-looking guy ever" was interesting and amusing, so I did some research. He would become the Saudi Ambassador to the United States in 1983 and leave that position in 1985 to serve as secretary-general of the National Security Council. Prince Bandar was the director-general of the Saudi Intelligence Agency from 2012 to 2014. Books have been written about him, including *The Prince: The Secret Story of the World's Most Intriguing Royal* and *The King's Messenger, Prince Bandar: America's Tangled Relationship with Saudi Arabia.*

In March 1982, Mom was planning a trip home when she wrote:

They're on another 'purge' here. People are getting sent home left and right. I may be seeing you sooner than June.

I think I told you that Dave, our boss, and his family left. He didn't like the way the administration is being run. I still like it here. Sometimes we get exasperated when we stand around in uniform waiting for the King until 8:30 p.m., and he doesn't show up until noon the next day. But guess we just have to accept these things.

My mom's position at the hospital paid well and allowed her to take one month off every year to travel. During the nine years she worked in Saudi, she visited 29 countries on four continents. She wrote in July 1977: "We're beginning to make our plans for our next post leave —

Greece, Turkey, and maybe Damascus."

In October 1977, she tells about the trip:

When we arrived in Athens, we didn't have hotel reservations, so the cab driver took us to a nice, new hotel that was only two blocks from the Acropolis. The room had a balcony so we could sit there and look out over the city and see the Parthenon. It only cost $14 a day and included breakfast... We had planned to go to Yugoslavia but instead took a 4-day cruise of some of the islands in the Aegean Sea.

Mom riding a donkey up a mountain to get to Santorini in 1977.

Mom describes visiting Kusadasi on the southern Aegean Coast in Turkey, taking a bus to Ephesus, traveling on to Patmos where the Apostle John wrote (actually, dictated) the Book of Revelation, then to Crete, and also to Santorini – her favorite place on this trip.

To get to Santorini, you have to take a tender (small boat) to shore. As soon as you get to shore, the land goes steeply up to the top of this high mountain, and it is up here that the town is. The only mode of transportation is walking or donkey. We took a donkey. I was scared to death at the beginning but as thousands of others have done, I made it okay. When you get there, you can see for miles. Really lovely.

In another letter, Mom tells about snorkeling in the Red Sea:

The water was quite rough, unusually so, so I only went out snorkeling one time, but I really enjoyed seeing what I did. I was tempted to ask 'The Man' to part the Red Sea so I could see more, or at least to 'calm' them. Since I wasn't an Israelite, I didn't feel that I had the right to ask for such favors.

On another post leave, Mom went on an African safari in Tanzania. She also took a two-week houseboat trip in Bangkok. While visiting India, Mom watched a silk carpet being made by four small boys. They sat in front of a loom with their taskmaster at their sides, intoning a song they all sang. Each note of the song told them which color thread to use. They were working on a "Tree of Life" rug, which Mom purchased. It hung on her living room wall for 20 years, and now it is in my home – a special reminder of Mom's adventures. She also purchased several other elaborately designed rugs in Afghanistan.

The hospital provided many types of entertainment for foreign employees in their free time. While in Riyadh, Mom took lessons in yoga, tennis, weaving, art, and gardening. She writes in 1981:

Started my art class two weeks ago. Painted my first watercolor – birch trees. I'd better stick to paint-by-number. There are three of us and one is very talented. I feel like a moron. Oh, well, Grandma Moses probably had problems when she first started, too.

Mom in Tanzania.

Mom especially enjoyed learning to weave. She writes:

I am into weaving, so I don't get anything done at home. Don't even get to bed until late because I hate to put away my weaving. My class this week was on baskets, so I'm making a brown and beige basket with a lid out of Bedouin yarn. That may be all you get for Christmas this year.

My mom loved gardening, so she tried patio gardening in Saudi. It was challenging, but she didn't give up:

I have planted some seeds and a few are beginning to grow. It's difficult to get them to grow. Have to water them so often and then feed them because all the nutrients are washed out by frequent watering.

Mom's Tree of Life rug purchased in India.

In another letter, Mom said she sold many of her woven baskets at the hospital gift shop and made more than $50. She had planned to sell some of her plants as her "next money-making project," but said, "They are so beautiful, I couldn't part with them."

Despite her earlier comment that her social life was "nil," it apparently picked up as she got to know more people. In a letter written in 1982, she talks about going on a tour of a farm owned by a prince:

Had a nice trip yesterday – about 120 kilometers out in the country. The VIP Prince took the dermatologist, his wife, the Lebanese interpreter and his wife, and two University of Riyadh professors to see his farm. He sent two cars for us. A Cadillac with a driver for the women, and then he, himself, drove the men in a Land Rover. He is such a nice person – very common. Yet when people greeted him (not us), they kissed him on the nose as a sign that he is a prince. He is a direct descendant of King Abdulaziz Al Saud, who was the first monarch and founder of Saudi Arabia. The Prince's grandfather, Mohd, was actually a more powerful person than the present king. Mohd would have been king, except that he wasn't well. In fact, he died at our hospital a few years ago. The farm grows mostly vegetables. As you can imagine, it takes a huge irrigation system being out in the middle of a desert.

Mom writes later that she was invited to a sheik's house for dinner, along with four other people from her clinic:

The sheik's home was beautiful – peacocks in the garden. The servants pulled some tailfeathers out of one for us so I brought a tail feather home with me. Two of the sheik's sons had studied in the U.S., so he spoke fluent English. Usually, we (the women) end up in the women's quarters, but last night we stayed with the men. Sat at a table (instead of on pillows on the floor as expected) and had a huge meal – really delicious. The sheik's family had been one of two families who first came to Riyadh. On their wall hangs a family tree with 3,000 names on it which goes back 1,100 years. Of course, only men's names are on the tree.

Mom also began dating. In 1977, a few months after settling in, she mentions a special friend, George:

George brought me a red, white and blue T-shirt (to wear to the big 4th of July party), Givenchy perfume, Oil of Olay moisturizing and night cream, (guess he thought I had lots of wrinkles), a really nice necklace – a Bicentennial quarter that has been cut around the head – very unique – and an address book. It was just like Christmas.

I'm not sure what happened to George – his assignment may have been completed and he went back to the U.S. – but the next year, Mom wrote:

I met kind of a nice fellow who is working on the new university here. Have seen him on a couple of occasions. It's nice to have someone take you grocery shopping so that we don't have to take the hospital bus which is always so crowded...

His name was Joe, and in another letter written in April 1980, she says:

Have been dating a rather nice fellow named Joe for the past couple of weeks. Am going out again tonight.

She continued to date him, and in February 1981, she wrote:

For Valentine's Day, Joe took me to the Marriott Hotel for a beautiful steak. Then he gave me another gold bar (ingot) – this time only a 5 gram one – a nice size for wearing around my neck. I didn't tell him it was my birthday on the 17th, so we didn't go out. His company just got the contract for an $8 million palace for a prince, so he'll be really busy. He had told me if he got the contract, he'll buy me two of the big gold bars and I could wear them as shoe buckles!

Mom said male/female relationships were mostly friendships because everyone would leave Saudi Arabia eventually. Some would be there only a few months, and some could get sent home on short notice. As Mom said:

If you're smart, you just don't form any permanent attachments because any of us could go home on 24-hour notice. It's just nice to have men friends to talk to so you can get away from the same old hospital talk.

Her relationship with Joe turned out to be more long-lasting, however, and he came to visit Mom after they both returned from Saudi. She even introduced him to her children and grandchildren.

Throughout Mom's letters written over the nine years she was in Riyadh, she talks about fabulous dinner parties, most hosted by American companies and some by Saudi royalty. She also mentions picnics in the desert:

> *Thursday night, four Saudi fellows, three male nurses, and eight of us female nurses went on an Arabian picnic out in the middle of the desert. No roads, but they seemed to know where they were going. They set up (before we came) two big tents — Oriental carpets on the floor and pads for us to sit on. There was a portable generator, so we had our own electricity. Stereo playing all kinds of tapes. We sat around and talked — they spoke fairly good English.*

Mom and her friend Joe ride an elephant in India.

111

At about 10:30, a couple of them drove back into town to get the food and came back with a huge metal dish with a lid to keep the food warm and a houseboy to serve it. First, there was curried rice with raisins, then on top was a lamb all curled up (all of him but his clothes, as one nurse put it). His teeth, tongue, everything. Whoever is offered the eye is really honored, but thank goodness, we didn't see that. We all gathered on the floor and ate with one hand. The lamb itself was very good, but I ate part of the kidney (I think), and it wasn't so good... Two of these fellows are very rich. One was a slave and when slavery was abolished in the 1950s, his owner gave him a million dollars and he started his own business. Very nice people – all of them – but very young.

My mom thoroughly enjoyed her time in Saudi Arabia. She made many friends – other Americans, Europeans, and Saudis. Whenever she heard Americans berate Muslims, she was personally offended. She said the Muslims she met were some of the kindest, most charitable people she'd ever known. Mom politely explained to anyone without a true understanding of the Islam faith the vast difference between the majority of Muslims and the few who are radicals and terrorists.

Ever the animal lover, Mom makes friends with a camel in Saudi.

Mom had varied duties at the hospital. She was assigned to a dermatology clinic for most of her tenure but also worked in cardiology, pediatrics, and orthopedics if time allowed. The work was interesting, and she made many friends through the clinic.

One such friend was a writer, Sandra Mackey, the wife of an American physician who was the director of the dermatology clinic where Mom worked. Very few people in Saudi knew that Mackey was observing and chronicling life as it was in Saudi Arabia in the late 1970s and the early 1980s. Western journalists were not welcome in Saudi and the government controlled all information that appeared in the media. Mackey had to guard her identity to avoid severe punishment in the male-dominated society.

She wrote a series of articles, published under male pseudonyms, for the Christian Science Monitor, and she later wrote a book detailing her experiences in Saudi Arabia. Her work had to be smuggled out of the country. A few trusted Western friends, who knew she was a writer and knew what she was writing about, carried her articles and book chapters back to the U.S. when they were on vacation from the hospital. My mother was one of those friends.

I found a copy of Mackey's book, *The Saudis: Inside the Desert Kingdom,* in our bookcase. Mom had given it to Steve to read, but I had forgotten we had it. The book is a fascinating account of the Saudi government and culture. It is also the source for some of the information I have included about Saudi Arabia in this chapter. In the book, Mackey writes about the small network of friends who helped carry her completed manuscripts back to the States.

I am amazed that my mom took the risk. Had the Saudis found Mackey's writings in her bags, Mom would have been sent to jail, or at the very least, banned from ever returning to Saudi. Mackey's identity would have been revealed, and she would have been punished for spying. Mom had asked me to try to contact Mackey when I was in Atlanta in 2008 for a work conference. She thought Mackey was working at Emory University. I checked, but she wasn't listed as an employee, so I didn't pursue trying to find her.

I tried again to contact Sandra Mackey after Mom died. I found a lot of information about her impressive career. I also found her obituary. She died in 2015 at the age of 77. Her husband, Dr. Dan Mackey, the head of the King Faisal dermatology department, died in 2019. I wish I had contacted them years ago so I could ask about my mother. I regret that missed opportunity.

During her vacation at the end of each of her 11-month contracts, Mom came home to visit her children and grandchildren. She usually brought gifts, including electronic hand-held video games for her grandkids. They're everywhere now, but in the '80s they were new to us and a big hit with the kids. Our son Aaron remembers, "I thought it was super cool that I had a globe-trotting grandmother who would swoop in periodically with exotic gifts and stay with us for a while."

I recently found a card Mom wrote to our son, Joe, when he was about seven years old. In it, she said: "After you left, I found the nice note you left in my coat pocket. Someday I'll quit wandering around the world and then you can come and spend part of your summer vacation with me."

Toward the end of her nine years in Saudi Arabia, Mom wrote frequently about coming home for good. In March 1984 she talked about her plans:

I'm getting anxious to come back to the U.S. to live. I think it's the first time I really felt strongly about it. I could leave as early as July 2 without losing two weeks' pay we forfeit by breaking our contract... If I stay until September 1, they prorate the two weeks forfeiture. Anyway, I won't stay until the end of my contract which is October 28, as I plan to spend some time in Iowa while the weather is nice...

At the end of her letter, Mom adds:

Billie (her roommate and good friend) *reminds me that if I stay until the end of the contract, I get my one-month bonus, and if I stay until September 1, I might as well stay until October 28. Decisions, decisions, decisions! Inshallah, you'll see me sometime!*

The Arabic word *inshallah* means "if Allah wills" or "God willing." The phrase comes from the Quran, the central religious text of Islam, which commands Muslims to use it when speaking of future events. Many non-Muslims also use the phrase when they are hopeful that something will happen. "Inshallah" became a natural part of Mom's vocabulary in Saudi, and she used it frequently after returning home. It was as if she knew she couldn't take for granted that the future would be exactly as she hoped it would be.

I got out Mom's letters from Saudi Arabia after she died – 30 years after she'd worked there. I had forgotten most of her adventures and am so grateful I kept them. I wish I had remembered the letters and read them to her when she was sick. She would have loved reliving that part of her history.

19
Retirement

We weren't surprised when Mom moved to Florida after leaving Saudi Arabia and retiring. She didn't enjoy the cold Midwest winters and loved being near the ocean.

We visited her at a condo she was renting in Perdido Key, Florida when our children were young. Mom was amused that while locals were wearing winter coats, our fair-skinned, red-haired kids were in their swimsuits playing in the sand. A few months later, she bought a house near my brother, Mike, in Jacksonville. When he moved to Dallas in 1987 to work for American Airlines, she decided to move to Northwest Iowa where her daughters and all but one of her grandchildren lived.

With financial pressure no longer an issue and after having had the freedom to do many of the things she'd always wanted to do, Mom settled into the role of grandmother to five grandchildren. Thirteen years later, she became a great-grandmother. Her great-grandkids, 15 in all, liked her sugar cookies, so she always had some in her freezer for unexpected visits. Mom started a state quarter collection for each of the great-grandchildren and gave them souvenir books in which to display the coins. Every time a new state quarter was released, she immediately went to the bank to pick up a roll of them. Mom knitted caps, sweaters, and slipper socks to give to all her great-grandkids for Christmas. Some of my favorite pictures are of her great-grandchildren sitting on the couch proudly wearing their latest knitted items from Grandma Betty.

Six of our grandchildren and Mike's granddaughter (far right) in sweaters knit by Grandma Betty. Christmas, 2003.

20
Sorry You Feel That Way

Day 17: December 28, 2008

I'm not sure exactly when it was, or what it was, that started us thinking about taking Mom home from the hospital. But we all – Susan, Mom, and I – arrived at the same conclusion at about the same time. For one thing, we had finally agreed to her doctor's recommendation that she be taken off the IV and given morphine orally instead. We would be able to give her a drop at a time under her tongue so she wouldn't choke when swallowing became difficult.

We had resisted any change to her pain management at first because the IV was working well. But Mom was needing pain medication every few hours, and often there wasn't a nurse available when she needed it most. We started thinking that we could give her the medications and take care of her other needs just as well, if not better, than the hospital staff. The nurses were caring for dozens of patients. We had only one.

We started making plans to take Mom home to die. The hospice director told us what she'd need – oxygen, a hospital bed, a ride home in a wheelchair-accessible vehicle, prescriptions filled. We decided on Friday, December 26 to take her home, but we waited until Monday to have her dismissed so that everything would be ready at her condo.

It's hard to believe how quickly we went from insisting she be allowed to stay in the hospital to desperately wanting to take her home. After more than two weeks at the hospital, the change of scenery would be good for all of us. Mom was excited and happy to be going home.

On the Saturday night before she was to be discharged, my mom encouraged Susan to go home and spend some time with her husband, Dennis. Mom said she'd be fine. She had even started eating a little – bacon and eggs, of all things – much to her doctor's surprise, and probably, dismay. Mom thought she was getting better. She'd had a bowel movement, so she couldn't have a bowel obstruction, right? She was eating and drinking. Things seemed normal. She was a nurse, and she had to know there's no "getting better" when an untreatable malignant mass is growing rapidly throughout the abdomen. But it made us happy to see her happy. Susan agreed to spend the night at home, get some clean clothes, and come back on Sunday morning.

I awoke early Sunday morning, December 28, feeling an urgent need to get to the hospital as soon as possible. Walking into her room, my first indication something was wrong was the strong smell of vomit. Mom was in her hospital bed, looking sad and weak. When I asked what happened, she described the ordeal she'd been through during the night.

It had been a mistake for Mom to eat solid food on Saturday. She said that during the night she became very nauseous and began vomiting violently into the pink plastic emesis basin. She turned on the call light, but before anyone came, she filled the emesis basin. She called out, "Help me, help me!" several times before the floor nurse and an aide finally came into her room.

The nurse said, in a high-pitched mocking voice, "I'll help you, I'll help you!"

"I know I sounded melodramatic," Mom told me, "but the emesis basin was overflowing and I was still vomiting." The nurse handed her one of the plastic tubs used for patient sponge baths and started to leave.

The aide asked the nurse, "Should we change the bedding?"

The nurse replied, "No, the cleaning people can do that when they come in," and they left.

When I arrived at 7 a.m. there were traces of vomit everywhere – on her pillowcase, her bedspread, on the chair by her bed. The red fleece Ho-Ho-Ho Christmas blanket the carolers had given her was wadded up and left on the floor in a corner. I picked up the blanket, and it, too, was damp with vomit. I walked into the bathroom and there was vomit on and around the toilet seat where someone had dumped the emesis basin. No one had made any attempt to clean the mess left behind. Obviously, the "cleaning people" hadn't been in yet.

I wondered if the nurse assumed that this very sick, 84-year-old woman on morphine wasn't lucid enough to know what was going on, or at least, not able to report it. Despite the disease and the drugs, Mom was very alert. And as a former nurse, she knew what the nursing staff's protocol should have been.

I was sick with grief, and I was furious. Knowing that anger is often a part of grieving, I have been asked if I ever felt angry after my mom's cancer diagnosis. I can honestly say the only time I felt angry during the whole ordeal was that Sunday morning when I learned how Mom had been treated by the nurse. It still makes me furious and sad as I write this account of that awful night. I find myself avoiding this chapter when proofreading. At some point, I will be able to forgive her. I'm not there yet.

I filed a complaint with the hospital's patient advocate weeks later, and she made the nurse send us a note of apology. The "apology" note read:

I am sorry to hear about your mother's experience while under my care and since then, her passing. More consideration should have been made to her and your feelings at the time. I am apologetic that you feel she was offended during her stay at the hospital. I apologize for any misunderstanding that may have transpired during her stay. I love being a nurse and take great pride in my work. May the next time we meet be a pleasant experience.

I read her note several times. I was not comforted by her half-hearted effort to apologize. I wanted the nurse to take responsibility for the patronizing way she treated Mom. She used words like "misunderstanding," and she said "I am apologetic that you feel she was offended," not "I'm sorry I offended your mother." I also resent her saying "more consideration should have been made" instead of "I was inconsiderate."

If we'd had any doubts before, the experience convinced us that taking Mom home was the right decision. She had been in the hospital for 18 days. If only we'd left one day sooner with happier memories of the hospital stay. We were comforted that all – *every single one* – of the other caregivers and hospital staff had been kind and compassionate.

21
Susan Dale McSwain

Susan and I were close in age – she was one year ahead of me in school. I enjoyed having an older, popular sister to pave the path through high school for me. Susan was tall and slim with long red hair, and she had a sense of humor everyone loved. Making people laugh came easily to her. She would try to make me giggle in church. She leaned over once while we were singing a hymn and whispered, "Maybe you should just whistle." Of course, I burst out laughing, which was what she was going for.

When Susan and I were young teens, singing together around the house, Mom once observed, "I think Susan is going to be the singer of the family."

Susan used her sense of humor when things were tense at home, too. If Mom was in a bad mood, Susan would say something funny, Mom would usually laugh, and the tension would be broken. Perhaps if I'd learned that skill, I wouldn't have been so anxious about Mom's mood swings.

Susan was on the prom court twice and served as a class officer. She could have dated anyone she wanted to and did. Tim, one of the smartest, nicest kids in the high school, went on to West Point. While there, he invited Susan to a

Cadet Ball. She turned him down, much to Mom's dismay. Susan seemed to prefer the bad boys. I once asked her, "I know you want to help everyone with problems, but do you have to date them, too?" She laughed. Occasionally, *I* could make *her* laugh. I referred to whomever her current boyfriend was as the "Juvenile Delinquent of the Week." She thought that was funny, too.

Susan's senior picture, Kickapoo High School, 1968.

After high school, Susan spent a year at the University of Wisconsin, Eau Claire. She was only there a year and then transferred to the conservative Christian college I was attending. Early in the first semester, she got in trouble with the dean for wearing short skirts to class. Faculty members would have female students get on their knees and if their skirts didn't touch the floor, the skirt was deemed too short. Susan almost got kicked out of school for sunbathing behind the dorm in a two-piece swimsuit. The school had many other rules – there were strict curfews, women had to wear dresses to class, men's hair couldn't come below the collar, and card-playing, dancing, drinking, and smoking were not allowed. The rules have loosened considerably over the past four decades, to which Susan observes, "God must have changed his mind."

Susan left the college after one year and transferred to the University of Wisconsin at Platteville. She was the cover girl for an edition of UW Platteville's school magazine, The Geode Gem. Susan enjoyed college, but she will be the first to admit she spent more time socializing than studying. She wouldn't receive a degree until years later.

The summer following her year at UW Platteville, Susan traveled across the country with college friends in a bright yellow 1967 Dodge Charger she and Mike bought together. She ended up living in Milwaukee where she met Tom. They had a daughter, Jill Elizabeth, born in 1974. Soon after Jill's birth, Steve and I convinced them to move to Northwest Iowa so Susan and I could spend time together and the cousins could get to know each other. Tom moved back to Milwaukee after a few years.

Susan and Dennis

In 1989, Susan married Dennis, an easy-going, soft-spoken truck driver. They both have a love of animals, a passion Susan shared with Mom. Susan and Dennis always have at least one dog and sometimes a couple of cats. Their elderly dog died recently, so they went to a no-kill shelter to pick out another one. Out of all the dogs available, they chose one that had been hit by a car and only has three legs. Sheba goes to work with Dennis in his truck every day. Dennis has a daughter, Kristin, who has two little girls. Susan's daughter, Jill, has two daughters and a son. There's nowhere Susan would rather be than with their daughters and grandchildren.

Susan's and Dennis's daughters, Kristin and Jill.

It was no surprise when Susan decided to pursue a career in social work. She always had a soft heart for people in difficult situations. For most of her career, she was a child abuse investigator with the Iowa Department of Human Services. After retiring from that position, she took another job at her local hospital working with elderly patients. All had dementia and many were dealing with depression. Susan worked as a social worker for 38 years and didn't retire until she was a month away from turning 70. She truly loves helping people, regardless of age or circumstances.

22
No Place Like Home

Day 18: Monday, December 29, 2008

The day we took Mom home from the hospital was a viciously cold day. The temperature was well below zero and the winds were strong. We thought Mom would be excited, or at least happy, to be going home. Instead, she looked miserable and forlorn. She was probably weak from all the vomiting the day before. She didn't want to wear a coat, but we convinced her it would be dangerous to go out in such horribly cold weather, even for a few minutes, without a winter coat. She reluctantly gave in and let us wrap a coat around her. I'm sure she wondered how she could be damaged any more than she already was.

A sweet young aide who was studying to be a nurse, one of Mom's favorites, pushed her wheelchair downstairs to the lobby and out the front door. We knew Mom was too weak to transfer from the chair into our car, and so a handicap-accessible bus was waiting for her. I was so sad — sad about Mom's awful last day in the hospital, sad because she seemed depressed, sad that every day was one day closer to her leaving us. I tried not to let Mom see me crying. I managed to hold back tears and thanked the aide for all she'd done for my mom. I told Steve to tell the bus driver that Mom was "very, very frail." I was feeling too emotional to tell the driver myself.

I rode the bus while Susan and Steve drove their cars to Mom's condo. I thought it would cheer her to see the outside world after not leaving her hospital room for 18 days. We knew it was the last time she would ride down Grand Avenue and the last time she would see Spencer, her home for the past 25 years. It was the final trip we would take together.

Mom looked so despondent and helpless. She said she felt okay, but I think she was in pain or nauseous. Maybe she was carsick from the bus ride. She stared straight ahead, not even looking out the windows, as I thought she would want to do. Maybe the light was too bright after being inside for so long. The bus ride was bumpy and despite having the heat on full blast, it was cold and drafty. I was glad we'd bundled her up. I began to wonder if she would survive the 10-minute ride home.

The trip was only about three miles long, but it seemed to take forever. When we got to the condo, we wheeled Mom through the lobby, rode the elevator up to the second floor, and pushed the wheelchair down the hall and into her apartment. We had to wait for the hospice nurse to come with the air mattress (which would hopefully prevent her from getting bedsores) before we could make the bed and help her into it. She sat in the wheelchair in her living room looking pale, dejected, and utterly hopeless while we waited for the hospice nurse to come.

Once we were able to get Mom into bed, her mood immediately improved. The nurse had given her morphine which works very quickly. Mom realized she could watch her squirrels and birds through the sliding glass doors in her bedroom. "This is perfect!" she told us several times. Months earlier, before her illness, Mom told us about watching a mama squirrel carrying her dead baby across the patio outside the sliding glass doors. It broke her heart.

Hospice Notes: *Went to patient's home today to admit to hospice. She just arrived home and is sitting in her wheelchair in the living room when I arrive. Daughters Susan and Mary present along with Mary's husband, Steve. After signing the necessary admittance paperwork, patient was pretty tired from the trip and wanted to lay down in the bed. We gave her liquid morphine as she was starting to have some abdominal pain, and once she got into her bed, she did quite well after that. She told me there are times when she has no pain after she takes the liquid morphine…*

… The family does not wish to have a volunteer, and they do not need clergy to visit them. They both verbalize good understanding of use of meds, of the controlled substance policy procedure, and of changing the oxygen from portable to the concentrator…

For about a week, Mom was able to enjoy being at home. She was happiest when both Susan and I were with her. We put a small camel bell she'd brought home from Saudi Arabia by her bed so she could ring it when she needed something. Her voice was weak, and without the bell, we were afraid we wouldn't be able to hear her call for us when we were out of her room. Mom used the bell often those first days. After hearing it ring frequently within a short period of time, Susan and I looked at each other with the same thought: Maybe the bell wasn't such a good idea! We joked about it with her. It made her laugh when we answered the bell with, "You rang?"

The first few days at home were good days. We asked her to tell us the history behind some of the things in her apartment – dishes, wall hangings, decorative items. She seemed to enjoy answering our questions. But there were so many topics we didn't cover because we didn't want to tire her or we didn't think to ask until she wasn't able to respond.

Mom was too weak to get out of bed, so one afternoon, while she was sleeping, we moved all the flowers she'd been given from the living room into her bedroom so she could enjoy them. When she woke up, the first thing she saw was a room full of flowers. She seemed confused. We explained that we'd moved the flowers in so she could see them. She smiled and said sheepishly, "I thought I was at my funeral!"

Susan and Dennis lived 40 miles away, so she stayed every night with Mom, both at the hospital (except for the night Mom got so sick) and at the condo. Susan slept on the sofa in Mom's hospital room and in a recliner that we moved into the bedroom for Mom's remaining days. I went home every night to sleep in my own bed. I was grateful to have that time to decompress and to have some normal time with Steve. I appreciated Susan's willingness – desire, even – to stay with Mom around the clock.

Mom had been home just two days when we started noticing that her preference for us both to be in her room at all times was becoming an obsession. One night, Mom woke up at 2 a.m. and insisted Susan call me to come right away. I wonder if she thought she was going to die at that moment. Susan thought she could change Mom's mind about calling us in the middle of the night by saying, "Mom, they're probably sleeping and won't hear the phone."

Mom retorted, "Well, they've got four phones!" Reluctantly, Susan called and woke us.

It was terribly cold and blustery as Steve and I drove the empty streets to her condo. When we got there, Mom asked us all to gather around and hold hands. We waited for 10 or 15 minutes, but nothing happened. A few nights later, she asked Susan to call us again after midnight, but Susan told her the weather was too bad for us to drive from our house to her condo. Mom never liked for us to travel when the roads were icy and so she didn't insist we come.

23
A New Year

Mom was happy to be home, but her condition continued to decline daily. Since she wasn't able to eat or drink, her face began to look gaunt. By contrast, her stomach became more and more distended as the cancer grew and spread. When I looked at her, memories of how Mike looked just before he died washed over me, compounding my distress. Mom slept more of the time, which was a blessing. Every day we watched and waited for her to slip away. Although she was accepting of her fate, she wasn't going to go gentle into that goodnight, to borrow words from poet Dylan Thomas. At one point she announced to us with her eyes closed, but smiling, "I'm a tough old lady!"

Although she seemed confused sometimes, Mom remained remarkably lucid most of the 16 days she was at home. On the second or third day, she asked us to call the local newspaper to have her paper delivered to her condo instead of the hospital, where it had been mailed while she was a patient. We told her the newspaper was no longer delivered in Spencer – it is mailed to all residents instead. She said, very firmly, "No, it is delivered here." And, sure enough, although the rest of the town had started getting their newspapers in the mail, residents of Golfview Condominiums had their papers delivered. We were amazed that she was so on top of little things like newspaper delivery even though she was no longer reading the paper. I think we underestimated her too often, thinking she was confused when, in fact, we were the ones who didn't understand.

Susan and I sat next to Mom's bed most days, or in the adjoining living room of her one-bedroom condo. Like in her bedroom, there were sliding glass doors that led from the living room out onto a deck that overlooked the municipal golf course. She and her friends were golfers, and the golf course was one of the primary reasons she moved there. In warmer weather, we could have stepped out onto the deck occasionally just to get a breath of fresh air. But the weather was too brutal to go outside even for a few moments.

Hospice Notes: *Went to Betty's today to see how she was doing and how her daughters were doing with her care. She is resting in her bed and is quite comfortable, she tells me. They are giving her morphine every two to four hours and that seems to keep her comfortable, and she has less nausea, also. She says she can control the nausea by lying still, not talking, and closing her eyes... Betty thought every now and then, she feels like she needs to take a breath but doesn't have any shortness of breath. I said we could increase her oxygen just a little and see if that helps. So far, the daughters seem to be coping pretty well and have a good understanding of what her care entails...*

It was New Year's Eve, and Mom encouraged Susan, Dennis, Steve, and me to go out for dinner. She felt bad that we were home with her instead of out celebrating. "You can hire someone to stay with me," she said. We smiled and told her there was no way we'd leave her, especially after the incident the one night we left her alone at the hospital. I think she was secretly pleased that we didn't take her up on her offer, and she was reassured when we told her we'd celebrate later in the year.

New Year's Eve came and went. Shortly after midnight, Mom awoke, and Susan told her 2009 had arrived. She cheered silently, raising both fists into the air in a victory salute. She was celebrating not only because she was still alive, but it also meant she reached her goal of surviving until January 1, at which time her Social Security would increase. She received just one Social Security check at the larger amount, but it was still a victory for her. She would never know we had to return the check because she didn't live the entire month of January.

Mom remembered that January 7 was her sister Alice's birthday. She was setting goals for herself. She had lived long enough to see New Year's Day, and Alice's birthday was only a few days off. She set her sights on her own birthday which was February 17. She must have noticed the glance Susan and I exchanged because she said, "Oh, that's too long, isn't it?" She realized she wouldn't be here to celebrate her 85th birthday.

24
444 and the Angels

Day 21: January 1, 2009

Hospice Notes: *Went to Betty's again today to see how they were doing and to instruct on changing the Duragesic patch* (Fentanyl, used for pain). *The daughters are a little tearful today as they are seeing some mental changes in Betty. They said it is not bad, but she does have some periods of confusion. They wish she had no nausea although she hasn't vomited. They said it doesn't seem to distress Betty at all, and they wonder if they're just expecting too much right now. I told them it is difficult to control her nausea with all the cancer and fluid that she has built up in her abdomen. Betty said she is satisfied with the relief she is getting. Betty said she was comfortable with the oxygen which we increased yesterday. She has no edema in her extremities…*

…The daughters said Betty slept five straight hours last night so Susan did get some good sleep, also. They asked if they should wake her up to do the gels (nausea and anxiety medication). *I told them I didn't think they needed to do that unless after about five hours she woke up and was in very much distress… I was very pleased to see today that Betty had no pain and that she did not think her pain was distressing to her at all…*

One day when Mom was comfortable and seemed to be thinking clearly, she mentioned the numbers "444." She would watch the digital clock when it turned to 4:44 and point it out to us. We thought maybe she was predicting that her death would come at 4:44. We asked her why the numbers were important to her, but she would just smile and, with her eyes closed, say, "Just remember 444." Several times over the next week, she asked us to "Remember 444."

We gleaned from her comments that 444 had something to do with angels. I wanted to understand why she seemed fixated on those numbers, but I was so distracted with her care and trying to prepare myself for her death I didn't pursue it. I wondered if she'd read something in a book about 444, or if she'd gotten the idea from watching TV. She loved shows about angels and the afterlife. "Touched by an Angel" was one of her favorites. Mom was not into numerology, astrology, or the paranormal, at least not that I'm aware of.

A couple of weeks after she died, I finally got around to googling "444 and angels." I was stunned when dozens of references appeared. I clicked on the first one, from Beliefnet.com:

444 – Thousands of angels surround you at this moment, loving and supporting you. You have a very strong and clear connection with the angelic realm, and you are an Earth angel yourself. You have nothing to fear – all is well.

I read it over and over again. I was astounded! It perfectly described Mom's last days. If only I'd looked it up while she was still with us so I could have read it to her. Somehow, I think she already knew what it meant.

The day after Mom died, I was looking through the yellow legal pad on which we'd noted every time we'd given her medication. There were pages and pages, starting with the day she came home from the hospital up until the day she died. Sixteen days. Towards the end, she was needing morphine every hour or two, and we worried about giving her too much. We shared our concern with the doctor on call, and he assured us she should have whatever it took to control the pain. Even so, it was a huge responsibility to decide how much morphine was too little and how much was too much. I counted the number of doses we'd given her. There were 444 entries. The last dose we gave her on the evening she died was her 444th. I couldn't believe it. I counted again: 444. I saved the legal pad with our notes.

In the weeks following her death, Susan and I kept running across those numbers. We'd be in a deep sleep, then suddenly be wide awake for no apparent reason. We'd look at the clock, and the time would be 4:44 a.m. Or we'd be driving down the road and the license plate of the car ahead of us included the number 444. The first time I checked into a hotel after she died, the room number I was given was 444.

A few minutes after I told my daughter, Laura, about Mom's fascination with the number 444, she sent me an email telling me to look at how many Facebook friends she had – 444. Years later those numbers keep popping up on receipts, billboards, license plates, digital clocks, online, etc. They often seem to appear on special days: our birthdays, her birthday, holidays, other times when our family is all together, or the anniversary of her death. Maybe I am subconsciously looking for them. But I prefer to believe whenever I see the number 444, it means Mom is thinking about us.

...For he will command his angels
concerning you to guard you in all your ways.
\- Psalm 91:11 (NIV)

25
Should I Tell You?

Day 22: January 2, 2009

Hospice Notes: *Went to see patient today to follow up on her symptom management, especially her nausea. Daughter, Susan, said Betty is doing much better with the use of the two gels together. They have not been giving the liquid morphine near as often either. They have used only three doses since my visit yesterday. The patient is staying quite comfortable and is very satisfied with her pain management. They did decide to cancel the hospice aide for now, as they feel they can handle their mother's personal care and she does prefer that they do it...*

...The daughters seem to be much more relaxed today, and they said they feel they are coping better and are prepared for whatever is to come. They said the patient did share some visions with them she has. She said they have all been pleasant and good visions, and they are not frightening at all. She is enjoying laying in her bed looking out the sliding glass doors at the squirrels that come up to eat and seems very relaxed and peaceful in her bed...

Susan and I were standing by Mom's bed talking with the hospice nurse when we heard Mom say, "Should I tell you? Or shouldn't I?" Her eyes were closed, and we weren't sure if she was lucid. We had no idea what was coming, but we had a feeling it was important – and possibly personal. We hurried the hospice nurse out the door as diplomatically as we could. When she was gone, Mom asked again, "Should I tell you? Or not?"

Susan said, "Mom, it's up to you. If you want to tell us, we're listening."

With difficulty, she haltingly told us she had gotten pregnant while in nurses' training. She had shared this only with an older doctor she trusted and the baby's father, who immediately left town. Mom said she never told her parents. She was certain they wouldn't be supportive. The doctor helped make arrangements for her to have the baby in Kansas City where it would be put up for adoption. When her baby boy was born, Mom got to see him only briefly. "I'm not sure he survived," she told us. "I think there was something wrong with him. His head looked too big."

Susan and I were stunned. We may have a half-brother we never knew existed. We tried to hide our shock as we calmly reassured Mom that it was all right and that we loved her. We asked if she'd like for us to try to find him. After a brief pause, she said yes. We promised her we would try, but she didn't know the baby's birthday or even the year for sure.

Mom was in nurses' training between 1941 and 1945, so that narrows down the birth year some. She thought he was born in the fall, maybe October, but she couldn't be certain. Although she didn't remember these key details, it was surprising that she remembered the full name of her baby's father. She never heard from him again.

It was several years after Mom's death when I was surprised to read in an old newspaper article that she attended nursing school in Eau Claire, Wisconsin after graduating from high school and worked at a hospital in Madison. Susan and I had always assumed she enrolled at St. Francis School of Nursing in La Crosse right after high school in 1941.

Why didn't she ever mention that gap in her history

to us? I started thinking maybe that year she had never talked about – the fall of 1941 through the summer of 1942 – may have been when the baby was born. Otherwise, how would she have been able to miss several weeks of nurses' training at St. Francis where she received her RN degree? If my hunch was right, that would narrow the baby's birth to late 1941 or early 1942, which would help our search.

Weeks after my mom died, I was looking at pictures of her as a young woman. There is a snapshot of her and four friends. The friends aren't identified on the back of the photo, nor is a date given. It appears Mom has a baby bump, but I hadn't noticed it before. My friend Leanne, a genealogy enthusiast, did some "sleuthing," as she called it. By looking at college yearbooks, she discovered that the women in the photo were classmates of Mom's at St. Francis and not friends from Eau Claire or Madison. If Mom is pregnant in the photo, she would have had the baby sometime after she enrolled at St. Francis and not the year before, proving my original hunch incorrect.

Mom, middle, with her nursing school friends.
She appears to have a baby bump.

After digging through many old newspapers and records, Leanne traced Mom's history after graduating from high school. She found out there are four months during which we can't find any information after Mom finished nurses' training at St. Francis and before she took a job. That may be when the baby was born, and it would explain why she didn't have to miss a large chunk of nurses' training for the delivery. It would also narrow down the birthdate to sometime between May through September 1945.

We will continue to search for my half-brother – not knowing if he even survived – hoping against hope we will find him.

26
Grace

Between Sunday School, church camp, and attending a church-sponsored college, I had a good start as a young Christian. I feel I've always known there is a God, but it was at camp where I began to cultivate a deeper faith. As a child, I thought of God as a somewhat scary cosmic Santa Claus, keeping a list of all the things I'd done wrong and all the things I'd done right. If the list of bad things was longer than the list of good things at the moment of my death, I was in (eternal) trouble. I have since learned more about God's love, forgiveness, and grace. There is nothing I can do to make God love me more, and there is nothing I can do to make Him love me less.

I didn't have the religious training at home that many of my Christian college classmates experienced, many of whom were children of pastors and church leaders. My mother wasn't a religious person, at least not in the way many people define religion. She believed in God, and she was baptized as a child. Mom modeled thoughtfulness and compassion by helping others – her patients, neighbors, the elderly, and anyone who needed more kindness in their lives. She encouraged us to go to Sunday School and youth group as kids. Mom usually attended worship services on Sundays, maybe because she wanted to set an example for her children, or perhaps she was searching for acceptance for herself. Sadly, the church did not always represent love, forgiveness, or inclusiveness to her.

As a divorced woman in the 1950s and '60s, I think Mom felt like an outcast by some of those who called themselves Christians. I remember one Sunday morning, when I was in 5th or 6th grade, the pastor preached on the evils of divorce. My mom was probably the only divorced person in the congregation of fewer than 100 people, and I'm sure she felt singled out and humiliated. I felt a stab of pain as she stood up during the sermon and quickly exited the church building. I wondered if she'd ever come back to church.

Growing up, I don't remember hearing many messages about salvation being a free gift paid for through Jesus's death on the cross. Instead, I remember hellfire and brimstone sermons – "Sinners in the hands of an angry God." (It could be that, as a young child, the sermons about hell are the ones that stuck in my memory.) Fear and guilt seemed to be the primary motivators for going to church, and church attendance appeared to be a major prerequisite for earning salvation. It seemed that one's chances of experiencing heaven were dependent on not breaking the rules. My mom had broken several of their rules, not the least of which was being divorced.

Mom sometimes expressed her dismay with Christians forcing their religion on others, missionaries in particular. I think she believed in one great God, and that people everywhere had some knowledge of God. They just called Him by different names.

I am troubled when I hear a Christian say something like, "My brother isn't saved." I believe that no one can know who will be saved and who will not. We don't know how or when the Holy Spirit will work in people's lives. The only salvation we can be certain of is our own.

In Mom's later years, while living in Spencer, she

frequently attended worship with our family. I'm not sure she was entirely comfortable in church, but she seemed to want to go with us. She especially enjoyed non-traditional services with a praise and worship band. On Sunday, December 7, 2008, Steve was asked to preach at an outreach ministry associated with our home church in Spencer. It was held in a building downtown instead of in a traditional church building, and the service was casual. We invited Mom to come with us, and, as usual, she accepted.

Steve preached on the topic of grace, singing the song "Only Grace" which beautifully affirms we are saved only through grace and not because of anything we do or say. I love the lyrics to the song, written by Kenny Greenberg and Matthew West. I noticed Mom appeared to be listening closely to the words which so perfectly describe that the only way to salvation is to accept God's love and grace.

Mom always enjoyed hearing Steve sing, but she seemed especially touched by this song. During the sermon, I noticed her reading through Steve's handout and taking notes. When he finished the message, he said Mom gave him a thumbs up. She complimented him on the sermon and song after the service was over.

Just four days later, on Thursday, December 11, Mom called us to take her to the ER. The next day, she was told the cancer was back and that it wasn't treatable. Thirty-seven days after the service, she was gone. We found her notes from Steve's sermon on her desk after she died. She'd taken them home and saved them. I am very grateful she had a chance to hear about love, forgiveness, mercy, and grace before she got sick and before she died.

Steve and I have talked about that Sunday often, even now 11 years later. I asked Steve to write down his thoughts about how he felt God worked within all of us:

Betty had experienced what it was like to be judged and considered inferior to other Christians. She could see the hypocrisy in the church. She also understood, as a nurse, the power of kindness to help and to heal, to offer and apply grace. But I don't think she felt she could receive that same grace from the church.

Without realizing it, Betty passed on what she knew and believed about God's grace and compassion to her children through her actions as much as her words. When Mary and I began dating, we had many discussions about the Church, centered around 1 Corinthians 13, often referred to as the Love Chapter. As our relationship grew, it was Mary who encouraged me to think about the love and forgiveness of God's grace.

I was a judgmental young preacher wanting to stand firmly with God against sin. Slowly, the knowledge began to sink in that only Jesus's love for us through his death on the cross could pay the cost of my sin and the sin of the world. I began to teach more confidently about God's love and forgiveness, accepting God's grace through the sacrifice of his Son as the way to salvation and recognizing that God's people are imperfect and cannot provide the love, mercy, and grace that only God can give.

I have come to believe that my deeper understanding of God's loving grace was a gift passed on to me from Betty through Mary. That completed circle of faith is a precious gift God gave me when they entered my life. How wonderful it was to share a message of grace with Betty that day.

Cast your bread upon the waters,
and it shall come back to you after many days.

\- Ecclesiastes 11:1

143

27
Now I Lay Me...

Day 26: January 6, 2009

Overall, we were able to manage Mom's pain, but there were times we weren't sure if the meds were working well enough. We were so afraid she would grow resistant to the morphine and the pain would break through. There were a few times when she seemed agitated and would chant, repeating the same words or phrases over and over until they became unintelligible. Was she in pain? Anxious? Was it because her organs were shutting down? It was distressing for us. We promised we'd keep her comfortable, but we were afraid we might not be able to keep that promise.

Mom was extremely agitated on this day. I didn't know what to do to help her. I sent Steve an email at school:

Susan said Mom slept pretty well until 3 a.m. and then was awake until 6, kind of delirious and repeating herself like last night. She woke up right after I got here doing the same thing. I think she was saying "I don't want to leave" over and over. Maybe it's because she didn't have the drugs on a regular basis during the night. We hated to wake her to give her medication. She said she had some pain but didn't

*want morphine. We reminded her that the hospice nurse said it would
help with her breathing. She took meds at 7 a.m. and again at 7:45.
She is calm now and maybe asleep. Even when she's kind of delirious,
she has very lucid moments.*

Whenever Mom became restless, she responded well
to music. Steve often sang the hymn "Amazing Grace" and
"Way Over Yonder" by Carole King. He also sang
"Tennessee Waltz" to her, a song she told us she and our dad
used to dance to. She would say "That's beautiful," and when
Steve would pause between songs, she'd say, "Keep singing."
It calmed her. When Steve wasn't there, Susan and I would
sing to her, and sometimes she would sing along with us.

As her cancer advanced and Mom became more ill,
we noticed her obsession with money was getting to be more
of an issue. She began to express anxiety about the cost of
her medications. We showed her that the bottles of morphine
were only $16 each and told her Medicare/Hospice paid for
all of her drugs. She told us she didn't want or need the
morphine. We thought it was because of the expense and not
because she didn't have any pain. We reminded her the
doctor said we needed to keep ahead of the pain and not skip
any doses. Now I sometimes wonder if she didn't want to
take morphine because she wanted to be more alert. I just
don't know.

Mom expressed anxiety about other things as well.
Several days before she died, she said to us, "Please make
sure I'm dead when they come to get me." With heavy hearts,
we reassured her that after she stopped breathing and there
was no pulse, we'd first spend some time with her. When we
were ready, we'd call hospice to send a nurse to pronounce
her. Only after that would the funeral home staff come to get
her. She seemed relieved and comforted once she knew we
had a plan.

Hospice Notes: *When I arrived today, Elizabeth is sleeping
soundly and looks comfortable. Daughter Susan reports patient had been*

awake for the last 24 hours, off and on. Susan felt Betty was having some shortness of breath and hallucinating quite a bit. She told Susan she was having dreams and seeing some things that were frightening her. For this reason, the daughters have been giving her morphine every 1 to 1½ hours and it calmed her down and made her less frightened of what she was seeing. She did arouse easily this morning when I went in to see her. She isn't able to stay with the conversation as well anymore. She tries to answer questions and then she cannot seem to finish her answer. She is denying pain or nausea at my visit... The daughters are coping well and doing well with her care and do not feel they need any further assistance from hospice such as more aide help...

The hospice nurses came every day, providing support but not patient care. We tried to be sensitive not only to the big things like controlling her pain, but also to the less obvious things such as keeping her lips moist by putting a wet washcloth over her mouth, making sure the bed covers weren't pressing too heavily on her toes, and pulling the bottom sheet tightly so it wouldn't wrinkle under her fragile skin. Because of the mass throughout her abdomen, she could only lie on her back, making the potential for bed sores a concern.

Mom was so appreciative of the care we gave her even in those last days. She would often say to us when we'd gently massage her back or give her the pain medications, "You're so kind to me." We'd ask if she was comfortable and in a dreamy voice, she'd say, "I'm comfortable. I feel good."

I jotted down a conversation Susan and I had with Mom on a white legal pad on January 6, 2009, just a few days before she died. She seemed to be floating on a cloud, very relaxed and calm.

Mom: *Why is Steve smiling?*
Susan: *Because he loves you and he knows you're going to a better place.*
Mom: *Yes! A better place. I'm okay, honey.*
Mom: *Who's going to win this one? Wait and see. Cancer...that's a bummer.*

Susan: *I think you are going to win, Mom. We're all going to win — all three of us.*

Mom: *Touch me, Mary. Everyone touch me. Talk to me.*

Mary: *Do you want to talk about your squirrels?*

Mom: *No. My kids, my kids* (holding up my hand and Susan's). *I'm still here.*

Mom: *You gave me extra time. Jesus loves me. Mike will come.*

Mom: *Now I lay me down to sleep. That's what I said to Mike...*

147

28
Terminal Restlessness

Day 29: January 9, 2009

Hospice Notes: *When I arrived, Susan and Mary are both present, as usual. They report they are seeing more restlessness and a little bit of agitation at times with the patient. They said she does a lot of rambling, repeating words over and over that are not understandable. They are not sure if she is uncomfortable at those times, and so they are giving her morphine quite frequently. They asked if there was something they could do so they wouldn't have to give her morphine so often. I will be visiting with the patient's doctor about this when I leave today…*

…When I arrive at the home, Betty is pretty calm and answers questions with one or two words that seem appropriate. She then does ramble off in her speech at times to where we can't understand what she is saying. She is definitely getting weaker and more lethargic. The daughters want her to be more comfortable than this. I talked to them a lot about the signs and symptoms we are seeing that we call "terminal restlessness." These are to be expected. They do continue to provide excellent care for Betty and are very attentive.

Terminal restlessness. Interesting term. It sounds like

it should be a sermon title. Maybe that's how believers feel, knowing this is not our home. Something permanent and so much better is yet to come.

Because God has made us for Himself,
our hearts are restless until they rest in Him.
                                        - St. Augustine

29
The Light

Day 30: January 10, 2009

We thought Mom was close to death many times during
those last two weeks. I think she did too. Frequently she
called Susan and me to be next to her and "all hold hands." It
was as if she thought she could will herself to die at a precise
moment when we were all together. She was ready, but it
didn't happen that way.

The last day we heard her voice was Saturday
afternoon, January 10. Earlier that day, I told Susan and
Dennis they should go out for lunch. Susan had rarely left the
condo in the 13 days we'd been there. Mom was sleeping
most of the time and so they decided to leave for a while.

Susan and Dennis were gone only a few minutes
when I heard noises from the bedroom. Mom was sitting up
in bed, tearing at her nightgown, and repeating the same
phrase over and over. I couldn't understand what she was
saying. I was terrified she would fall out of bed. I couldn't
believe that someone so frail, so close to death, had the
strength to sit up. She hadn't moved on her own for several
days.

Then I heard her say clearly, "It feels like giving birth," and I knew she must be in terrible pain. Steve and I got her calmed down enough to give her morphine, and she went to sleep. Thinking back later, I wondered if I'd forgotten to give her morphine when I gave her the other medications earlier that morning. It was the only time during her last days she indicated she had significant pain.

Mom seemed to be sleeping, or perhaps semiconscious, for several hours after that. Later in the afternoon, Susan, Dennis, Steve, and I were sitting in the living room when we heard her voice. Surprised that she was awake and talking, I went into her room and said, "Mom, do you need something?" She responded, "I see the light. I see the light." I told her to walk toward the light, and she said, "Okay."

A little while later, we heard Mom's voice again. This time, Susan went to check on her. Again, she said, "I see the light." Those would be her last words. Susan told her to follow the light.

You'll have no more need of the sun by day nor the brightness of the moon at night. God will be your eternal light; your God will bathe you in splendor. Your sun will never go down, your moon will never fade. I will be your eternal light. Your days of grieving are over.
- Isaiah 60:19-20 (The Message)

30
Before You Go

Day 32: January 12, 2009

Hospice Notes: *When I arrive, I note that the patient is resting in bed very comfortably and peacefully, but she does not arouse and is no longer responsive. The family said she has not responded to them the previous two days…We discussed what will happen when the patient dies. There is an impending blizzard starting this afternoon going into tomorrow. We're not sure anyone will be able to get to the home right away when Betty does die. The family is aware of that and said they would not be in a hurry for anyone to come. They talked about how they want to prepare her body and dress her for the funeral staff to take to the funeral home. I told them that would be very nice and acceptable, and the funeral home would be fine with that. I directed them to, as usual, use our emergency number, and people will respond as they are able and when they are able. They are coping very well and doing a very good job managing patient's care.*

Mom hadn't spoken for 48 hours, her breathing was shallow and uneven, and we knew she wasn't going to live much longer. Steve and I decided to stay the night in the guest room provided for visitors of residents at Golfview

Condominiums. We desperately wanted to be next to her when she died, all the while knowing we might not be.

At about 7:30 p.m., Steve took Mom's pulse and said it was strong and steady. She had been concerned about her heart over the past year, but it seemed to be working well. Susan and Steve went out to the living room, and I stayed at the foot of her bed. I heard her cough, or perhaps choke, and I went to stand by her head. Susan and Steve came in from the living room to be near her. Mom was moving her lips as if she was breathing, but she didn't seem to be taking in any air. I asked Susan, "What is she doing?"

Susan said, "I think she's dying."

It was the "fish-out-of-water" description the hospice nurses told us to expect – one of the signs that death is very near. We held her hands and talked softly to her. We reassured her it was okay for her to go. We told her we loved her and that we knew she loved us. Susan asked Steve to pray. While he was praying, at 8:25 p.m., Mom took her final breath.

Susan said I could turn off the oxygen concentrator which filters the air so it delivers the correct density of purified oxygen to the patient. The concentrator had been running constantly for two weeks. I hated that machine – it was so loud. To me, it represented death and dying instead of the peace and calm we all needed. I thought it might be annoying for Mom as well, but the nurses said it would make her more comfortable. I wished the whole time there was a quieter way to help her breathe. But when Mom no longer needed it, it was Susan, not me, who remembered it could finally be shut down.

As predicted, there was a major storm that January night – yet another blizzard, below-zero temperatures, and high winds. When we called hospice, we were told the nurse couldn't get to Golfview because of the weather. We said that was okay; we could handle things. Next, Steve called the funeral home. A staff person said they would get there as soon as they could, but it might be a while because of the drifting snow. The snowplows hadn't been out because snow removal would have been a wasted effort until the storm was over. We said that was fine. We wanted to spend some time with Mom before they came.

Susan and I dressed Mom in the almost-new pink silk pajamas we found in her closet days earlier. We talked to her quietly the whole time. "Mom, we need to turn you a little. Mom, we're going to put your arm in the sleeve." We placed soft white slippers on her feet. We combed her hair and gently washed her face. We had given her a soft, furry stuffed kitty when her beloved cat, Jessie, died two years earlier. We put it next to her along with Mike's old blue cardigan sweater, which she often wore around the house. I think it made her feel closer to her son.

Although the hospice nurse wasn't able to come to officially pronounce her, there was no doubt Mom was gone. We could see it, and we could feel it. Steve checked for a pulse, knowing there wouldn't be one. The form on the bed was not my mom. What we saw was just a shell.

Susan and I placed a framed photo of Mom on the lamp table next to her bed so the funeral home staff would see the real Betty McSwain when they came to get her. She was not the sick, frail, lifeless body they would see lying on the bed. She was a strong, beautiful woman who was loved and who mattered very much.

We had just finished getting Mom ready when two funeral directors in dark suits knocked on the door and wheeled in a stretcher. I was impressed that they dressed up for the occasion even though the weather was terrible, it was late at night, and only the three of us – Susan, Steve, and I – would see them. The hearse had gotten stuck in the deep blowing snow in Golfview's driveway. Despite the weather, it took them less than an hour to get there. We left her room while the men moved Mom to the stretcher. They wheeled her out into the hallway, covered with a white sheet. For me, that was the worst moment of the 32 days we had spent with her. It was our last chance to say goodbye.

When they were gone, I went into her bedroom and found one white fuzzy slipper lying on the floor. I almost burst into tears when I realized it had fallen off Mom's foot when they were getting her ready to take her out into the cold night. I dreaded telling Susan because I thought she would be upset that Mom left wearing only one slipper. But when I reluctantly showed it to her, she smiled and said it was "Mom's way of keeping one foot here on Earth." Susan kept the slipper as a memento.

Hospice Notes: *Received a telephone call this evening from patient's son-in-law, Steve, reporting that the patient had died at 8:25 p.m. He stated that she had died peacefully and seemed comfortable in her last hours. Due to the weather and no recommended travel, RN is not able to make it to their home. Steve thanked us for our hospice support, and the family was very appreciative that she could die in her own home.*

Mom with her beloved cat, Jessie.

31
The Final Arrangements

Mom helped write her obituary while she was in the hospital. It was probably the only extended conversation we'd ever had about her life and, in particular, about her marriage. She seemed very willing to share details and to participate in telling her own life story. However, we still avoided asking the tough questions about our dad. She was feeling well, and it would have been the perfect time to ask her. But, as usual, we shied away from the topic.

We did ask about dates – when they were married, his birthday, the date of his death. We were grateful to have accurate information and the knowledge that she approved of what we'd written. When Mom died, all we had to do to the obituary was type in the date of her death.

Elizabeth Anna Rosson McSwain

Elizabeth McSwain, 84, of Spencer, died Jan. 12, 2009, at her home following a brief illness. A private memorial service will be held on South Mountain, Phoenix, AZ, April 17.

Elizabeth (Betty) Anna Rosson was born Feb. 17, 1924, in Readstown, WI, to Albert and Ellyn (York) Rosson. She graduated from Readstown High School in 1941, and from Viterbo College, St. Francis School of Nursing, La Crosse, WI, in 1945.

Betty worked as a registered nurse at Gundersen Clinic in La Crosse before enlisting in the U.S. Army Nurse Corps in 1947. She served at Fort Carson in Aurora, CO, where she met Arch Dale McSwain (Mac), who was serving in the Army as a lab technician. They were married May 20, 1949. During their service, they were stationed at Brooke Army Medical Center, Fort Sam Houston, San Antonio, TX. They also lived in Virginia and Florida.

Betty returned to Wisconsin in 1950 and worked at Vernon Memorial Hospital in Viroqua. In 1959, she received her degree in Public Health Nursing from the University of Minnesota in Minneapolis. She served as the Vernon County Public Health Nurse for nine years, and then returned to the hospital where she worked seven years.

In 1975, Betty accepted a nursing position at the King Faisal Specialist Hospital in Riyadh, Saudi Arabia, where she lived and worked for nine years. During this time, she traveled throughout the Middle East, Asia, Africa, and Europe.

After retiring as a nurse, Betty moved to Spencer, IA, in 1987 to be near her children and grandchildren. She worked part-time as a proctor at Iowa Lakes Community College, Spencer Campus, between 1991 and 2000. Betty was an active volunteer, contributing her time and talents to various non-profit organizations and public agencies through the RSVP Volunteer Program. As a lifelong animal lover, she especially enjoyed volunteering at People for Pets. She loved golfing, bird watching, gardening, wildlife, and nature...

In lieu of flowers, memorials may be directed to Hospice of Northwest Iowa, Iowa Lakes Community College for the Elizabeth McSwain Nursing Scholarship, or People for Pets, Spencer.

**In Loving Memory
Elizabeth (Betty) McSwain
February 17, 1924 - January 12, 2009**

We had talked with Mom in the hospital about the final arrangements. She was adamant that she didn't want a funeral or memorial service. When we asked why she was so set against having a funeral, she said, "I guess because I don't think anyone would come." We assured Mom lots of people would come – all the cards and flowers she had received were proof that many people cared about her – but she didn't change her mind. We asked if we could instead throw a party and invite her friends and family. She smiled and said that would be okay.

About a week before Mom died, when she was still fairly alert, we showed her the pictures we were putting together for a video tribute on the funeral home website. She seemed agitated, but then suggested we should get her friend Donna to help with the luncheon.

We were confused at first until we realized Mom had

misunderstood us. She thought the pictures were to be shown at her funeral, which she had been very clear about not wanting. We assured her that the photos would only be on the web site for people to view. We would respect her wishes. There would be no funeral service. She was visibly relieved.

Mom and her good friend, Donna, during happier times. They made a 4-foot tall snowman a few weeks before, and the warmer weather melted it down to this 10-inch one. Here they are holding a memorial service for the snowman. Donna is displaying the snowman's cap and scarf.

32
A Classy Lady

The days following Mom's death were busy ones. We were grateful we didn't have to plan and endure a funeral service. We met with the staff at the funeral home to take care of the few details that were required with cremation. I couldn't bear the thought of Mom's body lying in the funeral home's cold, dark basement any longer than necessary. I'd never been in the funeral home basement, so I had no reason to believe it was cold and dark – or even if she would be in the basement – but I still wanted the cremation done as soon as possible.

The funeral home staff said they would have to wait 24 hours to complete the paperwork, but that they would do the cremation as soon as they legally could. They asked if we wanted to be present for the cremation. We declined.

A few days later the funeral home staff called us to tell us the cremains (what an odd word) were ready to pick up. We did not buy a fancy urn. Mom wouldn't want us to waste the money. As we drove away from the funeral home, I held the cardboard container on my lap. I told Steve, "This should probably feel weird, but it doesn't."

We took the cremains to Mom's condo and put the cardboard container in a sturdy, brightly colored Christmas gift box near the window where she had always loved watching the birds and squirrels. The box would remain there until we took her ashes to Phoenix in April for the memorial service.

Two days after Mom's death, we began the task of deciding what to do with her belongings. Even though she had a small one-bedroom apartment and not many possessions or much furniture, it took us several days to sort, box, and deliver everything to various charities. We kept only those things Mom had designated for the grandchildren and a few things that had significant sentimental value.

We received so many sympathy cards with such thoughtful notes. I saved all of them, keeping the ones with especially heartfelt messages on top of the stack, including these from our children's in-laws:

I'm so sorry to hear of your mom's passing. I remember that when my mom died you were the first one to give me a hug, and I really needed it. Neal was in the hospital, and I felt so alone. I wish I could be there to reciprocate to give you a hug in person and to tell you that you did a really great job of taking care of her and loving her and carrying out her wishes for her final days. That must have been so hard and a gift at the same time. God bless and comfort you. She was a truly classy lady. Kitty and Neal

Our thoughts and prayers are with you. We both enjoyed your mom so much, Mary. She was such a great conversationalist. I really appreciated all the times she helped me as a volunteer at the Creative Living Center at the fair. She was always so willing to help whenever I would call. I am making a donation to People for Pets because I know she helped out there and so enjoyed it. I, too, share her love for pets as I have had so many throughout the years. Our very sincere sympathy, Dave and Sharon

Many prayers are with you as you are going through this difficult time of grieving for your mother. Even with the sure knowledge of her new address, there are so many times you'd like to pick up the phone for a little chat or just stop by her house for a quick visit. I've had this desire since my mother's death 27 years ago. How grateful we are to know we can rely on God's promised presence and realize we will never be alone. Love, Ann and Jim

Steve's mom was 89 years old when my mom died (Doris lived to be 96), but she still took time to write this sweet note:

I always admired Betty. I felt she had so many qualities that I didn't have: Courage, daring, and dignity. I was proud to call her my friend. Love Forever, Mom S.

We also received many sympathy cards from friends and neighbors at Golfview Condominiums:

We want you to know that we are missing your dear mother so much. She was a very special neighbor and friend here at Golfview. You and Susan, and all the family, were such a blessing to her, and gave her so much love and comfort, especially in her last weeks and days. God Bless you all. We chose to make a memorial donation to Hospice of Northwest Iowa in Betty's name as they were such wonderful caregivers.

Mom always respected and admired doctors, but she especially liked her general practitioner, who had been her doctor for 25 years. He was the one who broke the news to her that her cancer was back and that it was untreatable. Despite her being so ill, Mom always commented on his fashionable shirts and ties when he stopped for daily rounds. He would respond that his wife got all the credit for picking them out, and that never failed to get a smile from my mom. I was touched by a card from the clinic staff which included this note from the doctor:

To the McSwain Family,

It was an honor providing care for Betty. Even when she

struggled with severe illness, she remained a delightful and appreciative patient. I will miss her.

He signed his first and last name, leaving off his title, "Dr."

Mom would have been surprised at the number of sympathy cards we received – there were well over 100 of them. She had no idea there were so many people whose lives she impacted. Many cards came with memorial gifts. Susan and I divided up the list and began the time-consuming but healing task of writing thank-you cards.

Since there would be no funeral, I went back to work just two days after Mom's death. I had missed so much time at my job during the five weeks we cared for her that I felt I needed to get back to the office. Staying busy took my mind off her for a few minutes at a time, but I wonder sometimes if I went back to work too soon. I hadn't had time to grieve. On the other hand, as I would find out later, my grieving process would take years, not days or weeks.

33
Letters to Mom

The business that follows a death began almost immediately. Mom had set up a revocable living trust and named me as the successor trustee, so I was in charge of distributing the assets. I took the responsibility very seriously as I knew how important it was to her. It helped that she kept meticulous records and had written down all the details we would need to know after she died. All her important papers were neatly organized in her white three-ring notebook. Even so, it was a challenge over the next 12 months to make sure everything was done perfectly.

I can't describe the irrational dread I felt the first time I walked into Mom's bank to handle the paperwork. For one thing, I couldn't talk about her without crying, but here I was explaining to a bank teller that my mom had died, and I would be taking over her accounts. The staff knew Mom, and they were so caring and considerate that it made the experience less painful. But still, every time I walked into the bank, probably a dozen times during that first year, I felt slightly nauseous and embarrassed at my inability to control my emotions.

I thought it would get easier as the weeks went by. It

didn't. I wasn't coping as well as I thought I would, or should. I needed a plan or strategy, maybe counseling, to get me through this. I started writing letters to Mom hoping that putting my thoughts on paper would help.

Feb. 12, 2009

Dear Mom,

It was a month ago today that you died. In some ways, it seems like so much longer. Anyway, I talk to you in my head a lot, so I decided it might be good therapy for me to write you a letter from time to time.

I don't think it has sunk in yet that you're gone. That will probably take a few months. When you were so sick, you were concerned about how we'd handle your death. You asked us several times if we'd be okay. We told you we would – we had our husbands, our children, and our grandchildren. I was wrong. I'm not okay.

In the first few days after you died, I felt mostly relief that you wouldn't have to suffer any more than you did. We were terrified that you'd become resistant to the morphine, and we knew that without it, you'd be in great pain. Watching you die was the hardest thing I've ever done, and it took a toll on me emotionally. Susan handled caring for you so much better than I did. She said taking care of you relieved her stress.

Now that a month has passed, reality has begun to set in. Death is so final. I didn't fully understand that phrase until now. My mind keeps replaying those last few days in my head like a movie. Susan is probably struggling as much as I am. But we will be okay. It will just take a while.

There are many things about the experience, though, that make me happy. Your obituary was nice, and I love the picture we used. I wish you had seen it. The one we showed you in the hospital that we had planned to use for the obit was taken several years ago. Susan didn't like it, and I wasn't crazy about it. I don't think you liked it either, but you didn't say anything when we showed it to you. I think you were just too weak to suggest we find another picture. In those last few days at your house, Steve looked through all the photos on our computer. It took him hours, but he finally found a nice one taken at the Readstown all-school reunion a few months before you died.

You were so happy that day to go back to Readstown and see old friends and relatives. I wish we'd had the picture printed for you before you got sick. As in the case of so many digital photos, we'd forgotten we had it.

You lived for a month and a day after we heard the final diagnosis. Not much time, but enough to get your affairs in order and for us to have some really good conversations. Every so often we think of questions we wish we'd asked you, like: Where did you get the anniversary clock? Is there a story behind it? Was it a family heirloom? Or did you buy it at your favorite shopping place, the Dollar Store? It seems kind of plastic-y, so I'm putting my bet on the Dollar Store.

Mostly, I regret not asking you more about our dad. What were his parents' names? Did he have siblings? How did you meet? We know so little about him, but it didn't seem to matter much during the last few weeks we had with you. It's beginning to matter more now that you're gone. I've been thinking about doing some online research to see if I can find out more about the McSwains.

I keep one of the funeral folders with your picture on the front of the refrigerator, one on the lamp table in our den, and another one in my top desk drawer at work. It makes me happy each time I look at it. I thought it might make me sad, but it has the opposite effect because it's such a nice photo of you. I have to remind myself that although the picture was taken just two years before you died, you aged significantly in those two years. Maybe it was because of the cancer, but you had gotten more wrinkles, your hair was completely grey – no longer a little reddish like in the picture. Your body was shrinking and your shoulders more stooped. If you had lived longer, you wouldn't have been happy about going through the aging process, and I know you wouldn't have wanted to be dependent on anyone.

I have mixed feelings when I hear "Way Over Yonder" or "Amazing Grace" – two of the songs we sang to you when you were ill. Now when I hear those songs, they make me a little sad, but mostly they remind me of how much you enjoyed having us sing. I am grateful for that.

Love, Mary

34
Happy Birthday, Mom

Although Mom was very definite about not wanting a funeral or any type of memorial service, she did give her blessing to a party hosted for her friends by her daughters. Susan and I decided to have the celebration on what would have been her 85th birthday, February 17, 2009. Another family party would be held in the summer when Iowa weather is more conducive to travel. I wanted to tell Mom about our plans, so I wrote another letter.

March 6, 2009

Dear Mom,

You said you didn't want any kind of visitation or funeral. We tried, half-heartedly, to talk you into a service. But to be honest, we were relieved not to have to plan and attend a funeral. When the funeral home staff came to get you the night you died, they asked us about arrangements. We told them what your wishes were (cremation, no service), and one of them said, pointing at Susan and me, "Yes, but what do YOU want?" At first, I was appalled that he thought it was okay for us to disregard your wishes. But I know that funerals are for the living and not so much for the one who has died. We told him, however, that we would respect your wishes. There would be no funeral.

Since you were okay with us throwing a party, we celebrated your birthday with dinner for your friends at Golfview. You probably would think we spent too much money, but we agreed this would be a good way to celebrate your life. There were 47 guests, including Susan, Steve, me, and Joe, Nicole, and their kids. All your neighbors from Golfview came. We decorated the tables with flowers and pictures of you ranging in age from when you were a teenager through your 84th year. We had a catered meal and a birthday cake.

People were so appreciative, and they said such nice things about you! You were very popular with the other residents. Remember the new couple at the condo that no one knew very well? He was bent over, maybe from arthritis or scoliosis, and he couldn't raise his head. His only view was of the floor and people's feet. His wife told me that whenever you would see them in the hall, you would stop and bend down so you could talk to him face to face. I guess you were the only one who took the time. Other people just talked to her about him, rather than talking directly to him.

Monday was another emotional hurdle for me. I cashed the first of your savings bonds – the ones that you bought 30 years ago. I realize it's a big responsibility to manage your trust, and I hope I'm up to the challenge. You paid $3,250 for the bonds in 1979, and when we cashed them, they were worth more than $28,000! Each of the grandkids got a check, along with a letter from Susan and me encouraging them to use the money wisely, as you would have done. The kids were very appreciative – I wish they could thank you personally. Even though we told your grandkids they should use the money to first pay off debts, I hope they had the feeling you'd be okay with them doing something special that they wouldn't have been able to do without your gift.

We have made travel arrangements for our trip to Phoenix where we will scatter your ashes on South Mountain as you requested. They're at your condo in a nice Christmas gift box decorated with happy snowmen. We put the box beside the sliding glass doors in your living room so you'd be close to the birds and squirrels and have a view of the golf course. We thought you'd want to stay at your little apartment as long as you could until it was time to be reunited with Mike on South Mountain.

We put a sign on the box that read: "Please do not move this box." We knew we'd have to hire someone to clean before we put the condo on the market, and we didn't want anyone to tamper with the box. As it turned out, Donna's daughter-in-law did the cleaning. She told Donna later, "I hope that was Betty because I chatted with her the whole time I was there!"

Love, Mary

35
South Mountain

Susan and I started making plans to go to Phoenix for Mom's informal memorial service in the spring. According to her wishes, we would find the exact location on South Mountain where we had scattered Mike's ashes eight years before.

It had been a warm day in May 2001 when Mom, Leslie, Susan, Dennis, Steve, and I met Greg in Phoenix and headed to South Mountain for Mike's memorial service. We drove to Holburt Overlook where we could see the city of Phoenix below us. There was a large boulder with a deep crevice about 200 yards off the road. We sat near the boulder as Steve read scripture and sang "Amazing Grace." Then we scattered Mike's ashes over the cliff, reminisced, cried a little, and left a Bible in the crack of the boulder.

Mom had been back to South Mountain just one time since Mike's informal and private memorial service. Susan flew with her to Phoenix the year before she died. They stayed with Greg, who would help them find the place where we scattered Mike's ashes. It was a hot day. Even though they had the pictures Greg took at Mike's memorial service to use as a guide, they weren't able to find the exact spot. Mom was deeply disappointed.

When we talked with her in the hospital about the final arrangements, Mom was concerned we might not be able to find that special place. We assured her we would – we'd take the pictures with us and use GPS. It was very important to Mom that her ashes be in the same place as Mike's. I hope she believed we would find it.

Mike's best friend, Greg, and Mom console each other at Mike's memorial service. Mike's daughter, Leslie, is on the left.

In mid-April, Susan, Dennis, Steve, and I flew to Phoenix, carrying Mom's ashes, still in the happy snowman box. We had a letter from the funeral home confirming the box contained cremains, but airport security still ran it through the x-ray machine. The four of us stayed at a nice resort. Mom had wanted us to make up for missing out on New Year's Eve parties while we were caring for her, so we had dinner, courtesy of Mom, at the hotel. Once again, Greg went with us to South Mountain. We found the location of Mike's memorial service fairly quickly.

As it turns out, Susan and Mom had been only about 100 feet away when they'd looked for it a year earlier. If only they'd walked a little further. If only it hadn't been so hot when they were there. If only Mom had gotten to see the place one last time before she died. So many "if onlys."

Steve read scripture and one last time sang "Amazing Grace" and "Way Over Yonder," the same songs he had sung so many times to calm and comfort Mom in her last few weeks. Using the plastic cups from our hotel rooms, we dipped into the snowman box and scattered the ashes over the side of the hill. We felt a real sense of accomplishment. We knew Mom would be pleased that we had found Mike's resting place and carried out her wishes.

As we walked away, we heard a lone bird singing in the tree above us. We looked up and saw a bright red cardinal. Mom said once she'd like to come back as a bird and so Susan had given her a ceramic cardinal while she was in the hospital. I had read somewhere, "Cardinals appear when loved ones are near." Susan and I looked at each other and smiled without saying a word.

We boarded our flight back to Iowa, and as the plane took off from Phoenix, I could see South Mountain out my window. It faded away, becoming smaller and smaller. I couldn't hold back tears. I felt like I was leaving her behind.

36
Her Golden Ticket

Mom never wore much jewelry when I was growing up other than her gold wedding band which she wore on her left ring finger even after she and my dad were separated. When I was very young, she sometimes wore a pair of earrings I made for her in Brownie Scouts – black sequins held in place by short silver straight pins and stuck into half of a cork ball. I'm fairly sure she wore them to please me and not to make a fashion statement.

When Mom took the job at the King Faisal Specialist Hospital in Saudi Arabia, she started buying jewelry. Gold and precious jewels were readily available in the souks (outdoor markets) and were very high quality. Most of the gold was at least 18K and much of it was 24K. Mom said her jewelry – and, in particular, gold – was her "ticket out of the country" if the political situation in the Middle East got bad and she had to leave in a hurry. Cash would be of little value if the government was overthrown, but gold was always accepted. Mom told us she didn't have much confidence in the U.S government to get her and other Americans out of the country if there was an uprising. She purchased many exotic looking pieces of jewelry: gold cobra rings and bracelets with ruby eyes, large gold pendants with engravings of King Faisal or the Saudi crest (crossed sabers over a palm tree), and various gold coins attached to thick gold necklaces or bracelets. I wouldn't have selected the pieces for myself, but they would sell well – and quickly – in Saudi Arabia if she needed to get out of the country.

Some of her pieces were gifts given to Mom by friends and co-workers she met while living in Saudi. When making final arrangements in the hospital, she showed us a hand-written list of all her jewelry. There were notes about each piece including where and when she bought it or who had given it to her, how much she paid for it, and other interesting tidbits.

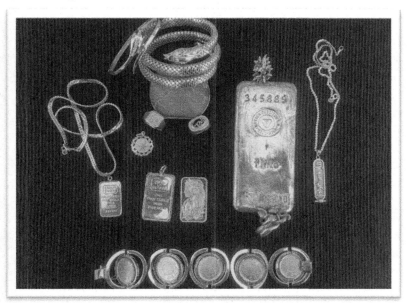

Some of Mom's jewelry investments: In the middle are two large ingots her friend Joe said he'd buy her for buckles to wear on her shoes. One of the rings spells "Elizabeth" in Arabic. On the far right is a cartouche she bought while in Egypt. "McSwain" is spelled in ancient Egyptian hieroglyphs. Pharaohs wore cartouches with their names and titles to protect them from evil spirits and bring good luck. Several pieces are decorated with cobras. Only royalty was allowed to use the cobra symbol in ancient Egypt.

I think Mom was proud of her jewelry investments. We never talked much about her collection, so I felt the need to write to her about it:

Dear Mom,

I want to talk to you about your jewelry. As you know, I've never been a big jewelry person. I wear the same necklace, earrings, and watch 24/7. I probably never seemed very interested in the things you bought in Saudi even though I knew they were valuable and that you were proud of your purchases. I considered your collection more of a burden than an asset in terms of dealing with it after you died. I wished you had sold it and just spent the cash on yourself.

I brought your jewelry home from our safe deposit box at the bank and started to inventory it. I showed it to a local jeweler who was impressed with all the interesting pieces. I started reading your notes about where and when each piece was purchased. With every hand-scrawled note I read, I became more intrigued.

Now I wish we'd had you tell us the history behind each piece. Not just Susan and me, but the grandkids, too. They would have loved looking at the jewelry and hearing you tell the stories. I'm not sure why we didn't do that. Maybe you felt safer keeping it in the lockbox at the bank. Perhaps you didn't want anyone to know you had that much valuable jewelry. Maybe you thought we wouldn't be interested in it, and that may have been true before you died. I think we assumed we'd have time for that at some point in the future. I'm sorry we didn't take the time. I guess part of it is we didn't want to seem like vultures circling over your valuables, knowing they would be ours someday.

Anyway, I want you to know you made good investments. Both Susan and I have decided we want to keep all the jewelry rather than sell it. We may not wear every piece, but it's a connection to you that we want to hold on to. I wear your cartouche necklace and your cobra ring with ruby eyes every day. On special occasions, I wear your tri-gold bracelet or your sapphire and diamond bracelet. You'll be relieved to know that we keep all but the ones I wear regularly in a bank lockbox.

We've shared some of the pieces with our kids and grandkids. I asked the girls to pick out something they liked since I can't possibly wear them all. Nicole Kathleen picked a thick gold bracelet, Nicole Maria chose three thin gold bangles and a ring holder, and Laura picked the gold leaf necklace you gave Grandma Rosson. I think it was meaningful to Laura since she was named after Grandma. Anyway, we've all enjoyed admiring and wearing your jewelry. It's another way of keeping you close to us.

Love, Mary

Years later, Joe and Nicole had a local jeweler reset a sapphire ring that belonged to Mom. The sapphires were real, but the setting was made out of some kind of mystery metal, not gold. After first checking with Steve to ask if he thought I'd be okay with the stones being reset, she took it to a local jeweler who took out the sapphires and fashioned three rings set in white gold. One was for their daughter, Ally, and one was for Nicole. They surprised me with the third ring on what would have been Mom's 96th birthday. What a thoughtful, beautiful and meaningful gift.

37
Jack's Project

I guess you could say I have been looking for my father most of my life. But it was a call from our oldest grandson, Jack, a few months after Mom died that prompted me to try again to find out more about him.

Jack, who was nine at the time, was working on a genealogy project at school and asked me for information about my parents and grandparents. I knew so little about my dad, but I was fairly sure his death certificate was in a box of Mom's papers. I found it and looked at the line where his mother's and father's names should have been. It said "Unknown." I had to tell Jack I didn't know what my father's parents' – my grandparents' – names were. He wouldn't be able to complete our family tree. I made a promise to myself that I would try to find out more about the McSwains.

When I did a Google search for "Arch Dale McSwain," I expected the same results I had always gotten – a few references to various McSwains, but nothing about my dad's family. This time was different. I clicked on a link to Ancestry.com, and a history of the Arch Dale McSwain, Sr. family popped up. I was amazed. I read it, and in five minutes I learned more about my father and his family than I had known all my life.

The history post begins in 1731 when the McSwains left Scotland and arrived in Pennsylvania and continues through the birth in 1893 of my grandfather, Arch Dale McSwain Sr., the youngest of 11 children. He and his wife, Rachael Stewart, had two sons. The oldest was my father, Arch Dale Jr., who went by "Dale" and was nicknamed "Mac." The younger son was named Warren.

Mac's parents, Rachel and Arch Dale McSwain, Sr.

When Arch Dale Sr. died of heart disease at the age of 42, Rachael and the two boys went to live with her mother and step-father. But when my dad was 16, he went to live with an uncle while Warren continued to live with their mother. Rachel died of tuberculosis in 1954. By then, both sons were in their early 30s.

According to the history, my dad was married and divorced before he met my mom. He had a son, Frank, by his first marriage. Frank had two sons, Robert (Rob) and Frank Jr. (Frankie). My dad's brother, Warren, became a Methodist minister in Texas, was married, and had three children.

The post was dated July 16, 2008, six months before Mom died. If only I'd found it sooner! Mom would have been so interested in reading it. She would have been disappointed, though, that a big chunk of my father's history was missing from the post. It says Arch Dale Jr. remarried but doesn't give my mom's name. It mentions him having a son (my brother, Mike) by his second marriage, but nothing about Susan and me.

Apparently, Mike had also been curious about the McSwains. I'm not sure how he knew we had a half-brother on my dad's side – my mom may have told him. I vaguely remember that our dad was married and divorced before he met Mom, but I didn't know they had a child.

Sometime in the 1980s, Mike and his wife, Jan, made the trip to Paris, Tennessee, where he met Frank, my dad's son by his first wife. Mike told me about the visit, but I remember very little about his description of meeting our half-brother. I was focused on caring for our three young children at the time. But I think the trip was rewarding for Mike. He sent me pictures of himself and Frank and their wives taken during the visit. When he left, Frank gave Mike two pieces of the McSwain silverware and an old medicine bottle from the McSwain Apothecary.

I was sorry to read in the family history that Frank died in 1998 – yet another McSwain I would never get to meet. I hoped to be able to find out more about his two sons, Frankie and Robert. I turned my attention to trying to contact the writer of the McSwain history on Ancestry.com, Linda, and also Debbie, who had added information to Linda's original post.

I sent Linda an email, but my message bounced back. Next, I sent an email to Debbie. I was amazed when I got a reply just hours later. It could have been awkward – my dad's first wife was Debbie's aunt, and I am the daughter of his second wife – but we immediately established a rapport via email. I am grateful to Linda for posting the McSwain genealogy and to Debbie for giving me a few more pieces of the puzzle that is my life story.

38
May Day

One of our biggest concerns in dealing with Mom's estate was selling her condo. The real estate market was at an all-time low, and there were several others for sale in her building. Spencer is a community of about 12,000, and the condo association required residents to be 55 or older, so the pool of potential buyers was small. We listed the condo with a realtor as soon as we could. We had already paid the $200 monthly fee three times while it sat empty. We knew Mom wouldn't want her money wasted that way. Finally, early in May, we got our only offer. I wanted to talk to Mom about it, so I wrote another letter to her.

May 1, 2009

Dear Mom,

Today is May Day. Remember how, as kids, we would decorate May baskets (usually paper cups with pipe cleaner handles) and fill them with popcorn and candy? Then we'd top them off with flowers we'd picked up on the hill. We loved taking the May baskets to our friends' houses, leaving them on their doorsteps, ringing the bell, and running. If they caught us, they had to kiss us. What a great childhood we had growing up in Readstown! I know times were sometimes tough for you, but as kids, we were pretty happy.

I will have to say that growing up without a father was difficult. (I now realize that growing up *with* my father could have been worse.) I was the only kid I knew of who didn't have a dad. But we loved our grandparents, and Grandad Rosson was the next best thing to a father.

Today is also special in that we might sell your condo in the next few hours. We're not going to get the $90,000 you were hoping for. Property values have fallen and the appraised price is now $81,110. The first offer was for $77,000, way too low, we thought. We countered with a number we thought would make you smile – $84,444, your age plus 444 for the angels. The buyer countered back with $80,900, and we responded again with $84,444. As much as we'd love to sell at that number, I don't think it will happen. At least the offer will be over $80,000.

Susan and I were both dreading Mother's Day this year. I didn't want to hear a sermon about mothers, and I didn't feel like celebrating with Steve's family. Instead, we went to Honey Creek Resort on Lake Rathbun. We had a nice weekend and even booked cabins there for our family instead of doing our usual Lanesboro vacation.

My friend Jane sent me a Mother's Day card with a note that read:

There are lots of years when Mother's Day for us moms feels like more of a hassle than a holiday because we are so busy coordinating schedules and figuring out what we're going to do (and when) for our mothers and our mothers-in-law. And then there's the Mother's Day after you lose your mom… Thinking of you, Jane

I'm so glad you were able to come to Lanesboro with us on our annual family trip many of the times we went. It was a good chance for you to get to know your great-grandkids better and for them to know you. I wish you had been able to come at Thanksgiving, just before you found out you were sick, but I'm glad you were able to spend that time with Susan's and Jill's families.

Mom went with us almost every year on our family biking vacation.
Here she reads the paper to three of her great-grandchildren,
Jack, Rowan, and Sam. Photo taken in 2006.

Susan missed having you sing "Happy Birthday" to her over the phone on Thursday. She had a pretty rough day. All these anniversaries are going to be hard, especially this first year.

There were two bright spots on her birthday. One was the offer on the condo. When Susan heard about it, she emailed me: "Yeah, Mom just needed to get to where she was going before it sold ...She's where she wants to be now." It was the sign that Susan and I had been looking for and hoping for.

The other highlight was finding a history of the McSwain family on the Internet. I had searched for "Arch Dale McSwain" many times before over the years, but I hadn't been able to find anything about our dad's family. I tried again on Susan's birthday and found a post on a genealogy web site about the McSwains that had been written in July of last year.

I wish so much I had found it earlier so I could have shared it with you. I'm going to continue to try to contact Linda, who wrote the post, so we can add our family history to what is already there.

Love, Mary

39
Sibling Therapy

For weeks after Mom died, Susan and I communicated on an almost daily basis, usually by email. It helped us both to talk and write about Mom – her life, her death, what we wished we'd done differently, and what we'd done well. I can't imagine being an only child and not having a sibling to talk to when they lose a parent.

We discussed handling Mom's assets and gave a lot of thought to what she would have wanted. Susan and I also talked about feeling guilty – something we both had in common, which was the theme of many of our email exchanges:

From: Mary Steele
Sent: Wednesday, May 27, 2009
To: Garvin, Susan
Subject: Mom

... I sometimes feel guilty, especially about spending Mom's life savings. I'm a little schizophrenic on that subject. Some days, thinking about the inheritance makes me happy because Steve was able to retire. Other times I feel bad about taking her hard-earned money.

I also feel guilty sometimes about not spending more time with Mom. I always used the excuse that she was pretty busy with her friends, but I know she would have changed any plans to do something with us. I was never completely comfortable when she was with us on a trip or even at our house. I was worried the kids would make too much noise, or she wouldn't approve of something that was said or done. Feelings leftover from my childhood, I guess.

I've been thinking lately that I wish we had talked to her more about how she was feeling those last few weeks. I remember once when she didn't want me to give her morphine, I told her she needed to take it so she could stay ahead of the pain. Now when I think about it, I wish I'd asked her why she didn't want the morphine: Was she feeling too groggy? Was it making her nauseous? Or was she just worried it was costing too much money? Instead, I just told her she needed to take it. She said okay, but she said it like she was giving in – not because I had convinced her she needed it. I think it was getting hard for her to communicate and she just didn't have the energy to argue.

I also wish we'd asked her if there were other things she wanted to talk about. I remember thinking it was too late – she was too sick to talk much, but then she lasted another two weeks.

It always helped to tell Susan how I was feeling and get her take on things that were bothering me. As usual, Susan had the perfect (and much less wordy) response:

From: Garvin, Susan
Sent: Wednesday, May 27, 2009
To: Mary Steele
Subject: Mom

I think sometimes she just wanted to give up and not take any medication. She may have also been getting a little confused at that point and didn't understand the reason for the medication, just that she didn't want to take it.

You spent much more time with her than I did. I called her, but not that often. I guess we can feel guilty for the rest of our lives about things we can't change, or we can be glad that the time we spent with her

at the end was very good, and that she appreciated that we were with her.
    We did what we needed to do, and I don't have many regrets. I think she was surprised at just how well we did taking care of her, so that makes me happy.

Susan was the maid of honor at my wedding in 1971.

40
Loose Ends

May 27, 2009

Dear Mom,

Today was Steve's last day of teaching. He has to go back tomorrow to check out, but otherwise, his middle-school teaching and coaching career is over. He's very happy about his decision to retire. It'll be interesting to see how he feels in August when school starts again. Hopefully, he'll still think he made the right choice. Teaching was beginning to be more stressful than enjoyable for him, and there are so many other things he could be doing. We'll just have to wait and see what those things are. We trust that God has a plan for him.

In two days, it will be our 38th wedding anniversary. Remember our wedding day? You were really nervous, and frankly, you about drove me crazy. Steve provided the calm I needed that day, and he still is a calming influence in my life. You couldn't have been happier with my choice of a husband. For once, I did something I knew you totally approved of.

We tried to keep our wedding costs low. The cake

was $100, the flowers were $100, and the pictures were $100. The photographer took 10 poses and 10 poses only. (We must have purchased the economy package.) You made my dress and the bridesmaids' dresses, each in a different pastel dotted Swiss. The church ladies made the lunch of little sandwiches, wedding cake, and slices of ice cream with a wedding bell in the center of each slice from the creamery. Altogether, I'm guessing our whole wedding cost less than $500, which was probably a significant hit to your savings account at the time.

Lynn Hardy, Debbie Olson, Bruce Ann McKamy, Susan, and Darcy Dorn. Steve's brothers: Phil, Tim, and Keith. His brother Tom was in the hospital.

With everything of yours that we give away, with every Savings Bond I cash, every loose end we tie up and cross off our to-do list, I feel like the distance between us gets wider. It's like walking down a long hall with the doors closing and lights being turned off behind me. I know it's just the physical things that we're letting go of, and that we'll still have a spiritual and emotional connection, but I can't help but feel you're fading away. Maybe that's how it's supposed to be.

Love, Mary

41
Remembering Her

I had been thinking of writing a book about Mom. The more I considered it, the more I thought it was worth pursuing. It would be a way to tell my children and grandchildren about Mom, so they wouldn't forget her. I struggled with the fact that she was a very private person. I worried that she might not want me to share details of her life even with family and close friends, much less with the rest of the world.

I decided to start writing honestly, authentically, and accurately, and I would deal with those concerns down the road. If I ultimately decided not to share the book with anyone, or with just our family, I knew it would still be good therapy for me to write. I wished I could share the memoir idea with Mom, ask how she felt about it, but since I couldn't, I wrote her a letter.

June 12, 2009

Dear Mom,

It's been five months today since you died. It seems so long ago, and yet I still think about you all the time. You are my first thought when I wake up in the morning and my last thought when I go to sleep at night. Is that normal? Surely, in time, I won't think about you as often, right?

I'm thinking maybe I should write a book about our experiences over the last year, Mom. I'm not sure anyone will read it, but at least our kids and grandkids will have a record of your life. I hope you would approve. You were always such a private person, but I think – hope – you'd be okay with me writing your memoir. I've been keeping a journal, and I have these letters I've written to you over the last five months. (When I told my kids I was writing you letters, I think they were relieved to hear I wasn't actually mailing the letters or expecting a response!) I've asked Susan to write down everything she remembers, too.

Remember when Grandma Rosson started to show signs of dementia? The symptoms worsened until she didn't recognize any of us and couldn't communicate. She lay in a nursing home with a low quality of life for ten years. It reminded me again how glad I am that you didn't have to experience dementia or disabilities as you grew older. As hard as it was to see you die when you were still so mentally sharp and healthy (well, except for the cancer), I know it was your preference rather than living until you were too old to function and care for yourself. You would have hated being in a nursing home, and we wouldn't have wanted that either.

I've been thinking about death lately, not in a morbid, depressing way, but with the realization that death is a natural part of life. Remember when I disappeared while playing along a dock on the Mississippi River? I was about four years old. The kids were told to stay next to the dock where the water was shallow. I either lost my grip on the dock, or I stepped into a drop-off and went under. You thought I had drowned.

Later, I remember telling you what happened, or what I thought happened, after I went under: I was walking along the river bottom. Instead of it being dark, there was a pathway of light in front of me. I saw the lower part of someone standing in the water several feet away, and I walked toward him. His hands were reaching out to me. I know it's not possible to walk underwater, but I can still remember walking toward those outstretched arms and being lifted up out of the water. The man carried me to you. I never found out who he was. I don't remember being frightened or upset.

I wonder if that is one of the reasons I don't fear death. That early experience is what I imagine dying may be like. First there's total darkness, but only for a second. Then there's a bright light illuminating a path to a figure standing in the light, His arms reaching out. He lifts me up, holds me close to His heart, and I am safe in His arms.

Love, Mary

You will not fear the terror of night...For He will command his angels concerning you to guard you in all your ways, they will lift you up in their hands so that you will not strike your foot against a stone.
- Psalms 91: 5a, 11-12 (NIV)

42
Second-Guessing

Months after Mom died, I started second-guessing our decision not to get another opinion after her hysterectomy. I wondered if it had been a mistake not to have her see an oncologist.

June 19, 2009

Dear Mom,

     I have spent the morning thinking and reading about cancer.

     A friend had a colonoscopy this week, and I know I should, too, but the thought terrifies me. I did some research to educate myself about colonoscopies, but getting more information has only made me more anxious. I'm already eight years past the recommended age to have a baseline colonoscopy, and with our family history, I know I need to have it done.

     While researching colonoscopies, I also looked up "malignant mixed Mullerian tumors." Sometimes I think we should have talked to an oncologist. Maybe a specialist would have recommended treatment. Instead, we just accepted the doctor's prognosis and let you die. But in reading about Mullerian tumors, I am reminded that there's very little that can be done once they have started to spread.

I read through the hospital notes I requested after you died – more than 600 pages covering your diagnosis, prognosis, daily assessment notes, and medical history. I'm about 99% sure there's nothing anyone could have done. Even if treatment had been recommended, I don't think you would have agreed to go through chemo and radiation again. Still, I wish Susan and I had talked with you about it more before you made the decision.

I also keep thinking that if they'd caught it just a little earlier, maybe it wouldn't have spread. There's no way of knowing that, of course, but I can't help wondering. And yet, I keep putting off getting a colonoscopy when I know that early detection is so important. Go figure.

Susan and I hope you'd be happy with the way we've taken care of your things. Cherish House is coming today to pick up several boxes. I think you would approve since they support single mothers. We've taken most of your clothes to Goodwill. Susan called last night to ask if she could have some of your clothes to give to a homeless woman living in a storage building. I know you'd be happy to share your things with her.

We kept a few of your possessions – the peach jacket we gave you that you're wearing in the obituary photo, the black leather jacket, and a few decorative items you brought home from Saudi Arabia. Susan kept your worn leather "bomber jacket." I think you had it most of your adult life. I wonder if our dad may have given it to you when you were both in the service.

I put together a shadow box for Susan made of items that belonged to you. I spent a lot of time deciding what should go in it and how to arrange it. I used the picture of you in your uniform and white nurse's cap (I remember how you used to starch it and then smooth it out on the front of the refrigerator to let it dry), your name tag from the hospital, the picture of you at the Readstown reunion that we used for your obituary, your gold earring (missing its mate) with a bird on it – since you loved birds and all animals – and dried flowers saved from the arrangement we had at your Golfview birthday party. I'm happy with the way it turned out, and I think Susan will appreciate my feeble attempt at doing something artistic.

This weekend is Father's Day. You were our mom and our dad for most of my life, so Happy Father's Day!

Love, Mary

43
Six Months

July 10, 2009

Dear Mom,

Sunday will be the six-month anniversary of your death. In some ways, it seems like it was just last week; but in other ways, it seems like years ago. I know I sound like a broken record.

For some reason, in my head, I had given myself six months to grieve. I thought the worst of it would be over by now, and maybe I am better. I don't have as many meltdowns, and I can (usually) talk about you without tearing up. But I still think about you a lot.

Remember I told you about finding the McSwain family history online? Well, I have been communicating by email with a woman on Ancestry.com who was looking for information about the McSwains. Her name is Debbie, and she's from Nashville. It turns out her aunt was our dad's first wife. The marriage was a surprise to most people, and it didn't last very long, she says. They had a son, Frank who died at age 42. Frank had two sons, Frankie and Rob, according to the genealogy web site.

I told Debbie I didn't know what my dad looked like. I'd seen just one picture of him that I can remember. It's a small, black and white photo taken from a distance. Mac is in the ocean with Mike on his shoulders. Mike is probably less than two years old in the photo. I'm sure you remember the photo. I still have it.

Debbie emailed a link to Mac's high school web site and his senior picture. What a surprise! Now I know what my dad looked like, at age 18 anyway. I don't think he looks like any of us, but I'll have to study it some more. Both Debbie and I are wondering if his brother, Warren, is still alive. He graduated from SMU in Texas, but I haven't been able to find out much information about Warren.

My dad's senior picture.

In the McSwain history, it says that Warren's son, Warren Jr. (also nicknamed "Mac"), died of Wilson's Disease. I looked up Wilson's Disease and found out that it is a genetic disease that damages the liver, causing cirrhosis. Other side effects are depression and psychosis. The cause of Warren Jr.'s disease was not alcohol related, but it made me wonder if my dad may also have had Wilson's Disease since he died of cirrhosis, and because it seems he had some emotional problems.

Maybe I'm just looking for excuses to explain why he became an alcoholic when he had a loving wife and three little kids. Still, I would have liked to have shared this information with you. It might have made you feel better if you knew there was a possibility that his drinking and behaviors were not entirely within his control.

Love, Mary

My dad, right, with his brother, Warren.

44
Like Mother, Like Daughter

I began to realize my anxiety was getting out of control. I did some research and, although occasional anxiety is a normal part of life, I self-diagnosed that I was experiencing symptoms of generalized anxiety disorder. According to the Mayo Clinic, "Generalized anxiety disorder includes persistent and excessive anxiety or worry about even ordinary, routine issues. The worry is out of proportion to the actual circumstance, is difficult to control, and affects how you feel physically."

That described my symptoms accurately. I had a feeling of dread, of impending doom, that I couldn't attribute to anything that had happened or was about to occur. I sometimes felt physically ill. The best way I can describe it is a heart-in-your-throat feeling that doesn't go away quickly.

According to MayoClinic.com, "The causes of anxiety disorders aren't fully known. Life experiences such as traumatic events appear to trigger anxiety disorders in people who are already prone to anxiety. Inherited traits can also be a factor…The risk factors include stress during an illness or a death in the family."

A few months after my mom's death, Steve had some worrisome symptoms that seemed to indicate cancer. It took a while to schedule the tests and wait for results. To our great relief, the tests showed no cancer, and his symptoms were easily treatable. And yet I continued to worry about him, as well as the health and safety of our kids and grandkids, despite the fact they were all healthy.

I talked to my family doctor, and I compared notes with Susan, who works with people dealing with anxiety disorders. I began to wonder if Mom may have had an anxiety disorder.

August 10, 2009

Dear Mom,

I have been having little panic attacks recently. Maybe they're not actual panic attacks, but they concern me. They're not debilitating, they don't happen often, and they usually center around health issues. I have become very anxious about my health, Steve's health, and the well-being of our kids, grandkids, and close friends. I guess that's a normal response to losing someone who was very sick. I think it's partly genetic, too, since you were always anxious about your kids, especially because several of our high school friends died in fatal car accidents.

When Susan and I were attending college in Nebraska, you worried about us traveling. Years later, you told us you cleaned the house from top to bottom to distract yourself. You didn't stop cleaning until we called to say we were safely back at college.

I've been doing some research on anxiety disorders, and I've talked to Susan. She shared some advice and loaned me some meditation tapes. I wish I could ask you about your anxiety. Did you think you were overly anxious? Did your anxiety ever lessen, or did it remain fairly constant throughout your life? What did you do about it? I'm sure you didn't take any anti-anxiety drugs because you didn't like taking any type of medication. When you had a headache or body aches, you took a baby aspirin.

Don't worry about me. I'll either get over it or learn to deal with it. And I'm not depressed. I told my doctor I didn't have anything to be anxious about – Steve and I have a great relationship, our finances are good, our kids and grandkids are healthy and doing well – and yet I'm anxious. He nodded like he understood and told me that's not atypical.

We had your "funeral party" last weekend. I told you about the one we had at Golfview, but this was just for the family. The weather was nice and everyone had a good time. We picnicked in the Milford City Park and then afterward, we each let go of a helium balloon with a picture or note on it that your great-grandchildren made. Sam and Benjamin told me, very seriously, they were pretty sure you'd gotten their messages, based on how high the wind carried their balloons.

It was good to see Leslie again. Natalie is a nice, bright, pretty little girl. I wish Mike could have met and gotten to know his granddaughter. I started thinking that this is only the second time we've all been together – all your kids and grandkids. The last time was for your 80th birthday party when we surprised you by flying Leslie and Natalie to Iowa from Florida. What a fun day! You were so touched. You told us you'd never had a surprise party before. Later, you remembered you'd had one on your 14th birthday. I've been looking through old *Readstown Specials* and other area newspapers, and I ran across a news item about your 14th birthday party. It even listed all the guests.

I lost my watch at some point over the weekend. I didn't know when or where I lost it. I looked all around where we had picnicked, but no luck. A week later, I decided to go back to the Milford Park to see if I could find it. It had rained twice, the grass had been mowed, and the picnic tables we used had been moved since we were there. I thought there was almost no chance of finding my watch. I took about 10 steps from the car, and, realizing it might be hopeless, I

thought, "Mom, if it's here, I need you to help me find it."
Seconds later, I turned, looked, and there it was, only a few
feet away. I believe you helped me – not because I needed the
watch, but because I needed you to show me that you're
always there looking out for us.

When I told Nicole Kathleen about the experience, I
said, "I don't know why I expected Mom to help me find it."

Nicole looked up at the sky and replied, "Makes sense
to me. She has a better view than we do!" Perfect!

The day before your party, Susan and I got together
to divide up your jewelry. I thought it might be difficult – that
we both might want the same pieces – but it went very
smoothly. She chose the pear diamond and I took the
diamond cocktail ring. I think we both ended up with what
we wanted most. We have some pieces we'll offer to the kids.
We don't have it all figured out, but we've made progress.

Both of us felt a special attachment to your bracelet
with the charms you collected from all over the world. We
thought a good solution would be to each keep a gold chain
and divide up the charms to put on the chains. Steve tried to
take off one of the charms, but it's like they're welded onto
the chain permanently. I think you're trying to tell us to leave
them all together, so we will. I'm planning to give it (my half
of it) to Susan for her birthday.

Something else happened since I last wrote that
would interest you. I have continued to search for
information about the McSwains and ran across the obituary
for our dad's brother, Warren, and his wife, June. They both
died in San Antonio in 2006. Coincidentally, Steve and I were
in San Antonio in 2006 for the Alamo Bowl. I'll keep looking
for information and will keep you posted.

It has been almost seven months since you died, and I
think that, finally, it is getting a little better for Susan and me.
I don't get weepy as often. At first, it was every day, and
sometimes several times a day. Now it is more like every
couple of weeks. I guess that is a good thing. It's not that
we're forgetting you. It's just that it's too painful to remember

so clearly for so long. Does that make sense? I think you'd understand, having lost not only your parents and brother but also your husband and son, although I'm not sure you ever got over losing Mike. I don't think we'll ever get over losing you, but the pain is starting to ease.

Love, Mary

We had a second party for Mom in the summer just for the family. All her kids, grandkids, and great-grandkids (one was not yet born) attended.

45
Finding Cynthia

Almost all the information about the McSwain family I found on Ancestry.com was new to me. But what interested me most was learning that my dad's brother, Warren, had three children – a daughter and two sons. It never occurred to me that I might have first cousins on the McSwain side.

I was especially motivated to find out more about Warren's daughter, Cynthia, who would be about my age. I googled her name, and I was pleasantly surprised to find several references for Cynthia McSwain.

The fact that Cynthia kept her maiden name, and that she was a published author, made it easier to find her online. I learned that Cynthia and her husband, Orion White, were both university professors. They wrote books together under the pseudonym O.C. McSwite.

I also found a link to a yoga school in San Antonio, Texas, where Cynthia taught yoga and developed a certification program for yoga instructors after retiring from the university. There was a photo of her with the story.

One last reference was for LinkedIn. I had never used LinkedIn before – I wasn't even sure what it was – but it allowed me to send an email directly to Cynthia. I had no idea

My first cousin, Cynthia McSwain.

if the email address was current, or if she'd read it when she got it, but I had to try.

On August 4, 2009, after several revisions, I sent this email to Cynthia:

Cynthia,

My name is Mary McSwain Steele. My father, Arch Dale McSwain Jr. (Mac), was, I think, your father's brother. If you are not Warren S. McSwain's daughter, please ignore this message. :-)

My mother, Elizabeth Rosson McSwain, was Dale's second wife. They had three children (my sister, Susan, my brother, Michael, who died in 2001, and myself). My parents were separated when I was 3 or 4, and I never saw my dad after age 6 or so. They were divorced a few years later, and he died when I was 11. We never knew anything about the McSwains — it made Mom sad to talk about my dad, so we didn't ask her many questions. I don't think my mother ever met my dad's parents, but I think she knew his brother, Warren (your dad?).

My mother recently died, and I felt a need to try to find

206

information about the McSwains. I ran across a post on Ancestry.com, and I learned more about my father's family than I have known all my life.

Don't feel you have to respond, but if you'd like to confirm that you're Warren's daughter, I'd be thrilled to have made contact with a cousin I've never known or met.

Mary Steele

Within 24 hours, I was delighted to receive the following reply from Cynthia:

August 5, 2009

Dear Mary,

Your email was a wonderful and utter shock. Yes, I am your cousin, Cynthia June McSwain, daughter of Warren Stewart McSwain and June Ruth Simmons. I am so happy to hear from you. It's a little hard to know where to begin.

I may have met your dad, Dale, but I don't think so. He and my father were somewhat estranged. They were separated after their father died which was when my father was 11. My father went to live with their mother, Rachel, on the farm that Rachel's mother and her step-father owned. Apparently, our fathers' step-grandfather was an awful man who made my father's childhood dreadful.

Your father stayed away from the whole situation, living with the McSwains in town. Our grandmother, Rachel, contracted TB, and my father ended up taking care of her. She died in a sanitarium in Tennessee in 1954, when I was 6. I was told that your father was an alcoholic and a "wastrel" (quaint word). He died in Florida sometime obviously after your parents' divorce. I have a memory that my father went down to Florida to try to help him but came back convinced that he was beyond any assistance. It was a very bitter and unhappy situation.

I never knew that he had any children by any marriage until a few years ago when I, too, read about our family and realized that he had been married twice. The write-up I read, though, did not mention you or your siblings.

My father was completely estranged from his entire family and rarely even talked about them. I have never met any relatives from that side of the family… I now know lots more but that's for later. My father went to graduate school at Southern Methodist University and that took them to Texas. All of us were born here in Texas and grew up in San Antonio.

My father and mother both died in 2006. There were three of us children, Cynthia, Warren, Jr. (Mac), and John. Mac died in 1985 from Wilson's disease which is genetic and about which we ought to correspond. John is 54 and lives in Virginia, owning a restaurant on Lake Anna. He is married to Linda who has three children from a previous marriage; they have no children together. I am married to Orion White; we'll celebrate 25 years this Christmas.

We are both university professors, retired now. Orion was at Virginia Tech and I was at the George Washington University. We lived in the Washington, DC, area for 30 or so years and retired back to San Antonio in 2003 to help with my parents. Orion is also from Texas and has lots of family here as well.

My father died of COPD, emphysema, etc., in August 2006, after a long fight. My mother died very suddenly and totally unexpectedly 12 weeks later of a Parkinson's complicated pneumonia. It was quite a shock. Orion and I don't have any children either although he has two from his previous marriage. This means that John and I are really "it" for our side of the family.

I realize that I have gone on way too long and you perhaps don't want to know all of this.

I would love to be in contact with you and will wait to hear further. What a wonder to have contact with a cousin. I am very interested in your life and whatever you wish to communicate.

Take care,
Cynthia, your cousin

I wish so much that I could share Cynthia's letter with Mom. I am certain Mom and Cynthia would have enjoyed getting to know each other. I also think my mom would have opened up to Cynthia about Mac, and I would have learned answers to questions about my dad that I was always reluctant to ask.

My dad's brother, Warren Sr., visits his mother, Rachel, in the TB sanitarium with his wife, June, and their daughter, Cynthia.

46
Life Goes On

September 10, 2009

Dear Mom,

 Tomorrow is September 11, the anniversary of the terrorist attack on the Twin Towers. You were the first one to tell me about the attack. You were working at the college and came down the hall to my office and told me you saw the planes crashing into the World Trade Center on TV. I thought it sounded like just another plane crash and wasn't terribly concerned about it. Over the next few hours, we began to realize it was so much more than just another plane crash.

 It has been almost eight months since your death; nine months since the night you called Steve and me saying you had stomach pains and nausea and asked us to take you to the hospital. We thought you had adhesions again, like the time a couple of months earlier. We were wrong. It's still really hard to believe that you're gone. Some days I think I'm doing better, and other days I can't believe how sad I still feel.

 We are getting ready to go to California with friends,

Tom and Margo. I'm starting to worry about traveling – I'm sure it'll be a great trip, but I worry about being safe and about getting around in unfamiliar territory. This worrying thing is in my genes – you were the queen of worriers!

Steve is enjoying being retired. As we told you when you were in the hospital, he wouldn't have been able to retire this year if it hadn't been for the inheritance, and we both are grateful. I didn't realize how much pressure he felt teaching over the last few years, mostly due to his hearing loss and one difficult administrator. He still enjoyed teaching middle schoolers. Steve says that if retirement has a downside, he hasn't found it yet. He has been asked to teach Earth Science classes part-time at Iowa Lakes Community College and is looking forward to that. I will wait a few years before retiring. I like my job, and the decision to retire will be a difficult one for me.

I have taken care of about 80% of your affairs. We're still trying to figure out the IRA, and we have two batches of savings bonds left to cash. We'll have to do your taxes after the first of the year. There's so much to learn and try to understand even though your notes in the white binder helped a lot. Don't worry – we'll get it done.

Love, Mary

47
Losing Her Again

November 2009 was a difficult month. I was dreading the holidays which were followed closely by the first anniversary of Mom's death.

I received an invitation to the Iowa Lakes Community College scholarship reception, which I thought might be the one bright spot in the month. Steve and I drove to the Estherville campus to meet the first recipient of the Elizabeth McSwain Nursing Scholarship, but the student didn't show up. I found out later she had withdrawn from two of her three classes, so she didn't even qualify for the scholarship. To make matters worse, the Foundation staff said they hadn't received my RSVP, so they didn't have name tags or a table for us. It was very disappointing considering we had hoped this would be an important part of Mom's legacy.

A couple of weeks after the reception, Steve and I were headed to Des Moines so I could attend work-related meetings the next day. We stopped in Ames to take our grandson, Sam, on an outing to celebrate his 6th birthday. We went to a pottery shop and then we attended an Iowa State basketball game.

After taking Sam home at about 8 p.m., Steve and I

continued to Des Moines. We traveled for about 20 minutes when we witnessed a car crash. The car crossed three lanes of traffic in front of us and then went into the ditch and up an embankment. We pulled off onto the shoulder, Steve called 911, and then he hurried to the crash site.

I got out of our car to see if I could help. I saw emergency vehicles approaching, but they went on past the accident site, so I ran along the side of the interstate in the dark, cars whizzing by me, trying to flag them down. The emergency vehicles eventually turned around and came back. Steve and I waited for the police to arrive, gave our statement, and headed for our hotel in Des Moines. Or at least, that's what Steve tells me. I remember very little about that night.

When we got to the hotel parking lot, I couldn't remember why we were there. I told Steve several times, "I think I'm having a TIA." (A transient ischemic attack, which causes temporary stroke-like symptoms and memory loss.) "Mom had a TIA in Saudi Arabia." I thought if we waited, and if we just talked about it for a while, I'd figure it out.

Steve checked my eyes for signs of a concussion and felt for lumps on my head. He thought I may have fallen and hit my head when I ran along the interstate to flag down emergency vehicles in the dark. My pupils weren't dilated, my speech was normal, and I had no bumps or bruises. However, I had no memory of the previous 4-6 hours, and I didn't know why we were in a hotel parking lot in Des Moines. After about 45 minutes, Steve says he somehow convinced me that we needed to go to the ER. He called our son Aaron, who lives about 40 miles from Des Moines, to let him know what was happening.

I remember looking at the ER clock at 1:10 a.m., which is when Aaron arrived at the hospital. Seeing him was the first new memory I was able to retain. Even then, I was still repeating myself, asking the same series of questions over and over. The doctor ordered a CT scan. In the three hours it took to get the results, Steve said he was "pretty scared."

Even if the test results showed the diagnosis wasn't life-threatening, he was concerned it could be life-changing for both of us. He told me later he thought he might be spending his retirement taking care of me for the rest of my life.

I had a couple of panicky moments, too, but for the most part, I was "calm and cooperative" according to Steve and confirmed by the doctor's notes. When Steve told me I'd had a CT scan, I wondered if I might have a brain tumor and briefly felt a rush of terror.

The CT scan and all other tests came back normal. I joked, "How would they be able to tell if my brain was normal?" I repeated that same question several times, which I'm told I thought was hilarious. After hearing the line many times, Aaron whispered to Steve, "Mom needs to get some new material."

As I was coming out of my fog, it occurred to me that there was something about Mom I needed to remember. It was important. What was it? Had I told her we'd let her know when we got to Des Moines? I hoped not, because she would worry if she was expecting to hear from us and we hadn't checked in with her yet. She would think we were "in a ditch somewhere."

Or was something wrong with her? Was she ill? Was she in the hospital? I thought hard for a minute or two, with a feeling of dread building in my chest. Then slowly I started to remember. She had been in the hospital and was very sick. Then she was at home, but she kept getting worse. That's when it hit me – she died. It was like losing her again. I tried to choke back a sob.

I was mostly back to normal by 4:30 a.m., except I had only brief flashes of memory from the previous eight hours. The diagnosis was transient global amnesia (TGA), and mine was a classic case. According to the neurologist, there are no lasting side effects except for the memory loss during those hours which I will probably never get back. I was relieved to learn it is highly unlikely it will happen again. It was the best possible diagnosis considering the scary symptoms.

The doctors said it might have been brought on by the trauma of witnessing the car accident, although the passengers in the car weren't seriously injured and so it shouldn't have been all that traumatic. Grief and stress may have played a part in causing the TGA. Or, the event could have been triggered by the physical exertion of running along the interstate to get help. They kept me until noon for observation and then dismissed me. I haven't had any related problems since.

As we got to the end of November, both Susan and I were dreading the holidays. She turned down our invitation to get together for Thanksgiving. When I got out Christmas decorations, I found the red Ho-Ho-Ho fleece blanket the carolers gave Mom in the hospital on Christmas Eve. It brought back all the memories, good and bad, of the previous December. I put it back in the closet. I wasn't ready to look at it.

I wrote in my journal:

Overall, I have been doing better. I don't obsess quite so much. I'm reading a book recommended by my co-worker, Susan, about the brain and how it works, which helps me realize I have a choice about how I feel. I'm sure I'll have bad times — especially now that we're getting close to the holidays and also to the anniversaries of Mom's diagnosis, illness, and death. But I'm also looking forward to good times.

48
First Christmas Without Her

I continued writing letters to Mom, though not as frequently as when I first started in February. I thought the fact I wasn't writing to her as often was a sign I was finally healing.

December 22, 2009

Dear Mom,

A year ago today, you were spending your 11th day in the hospital. The days were long, but you made it easier for us by being calm and accepting. At first, you wanted to stay in the hospital to die, and Susan and I agreed that would be best. We didn't know if we could take care of you by ourselves. But as the days passed, we realized we could give you one-on-one care and so we decided to take you home.

When I think of where we were a year ago, I am so thankful it is behind us. That sounds selfish, but my anxiety was almost unbearable sometimes. Going home every night helped me get through those long days. Susan did so much better than I did. She didn't want to leave you even for a few hours. She was such a good caregiver.

Susan is having a difficult time with the holidays. It hasn't been as bad for me as for her. I've been staying busy, which helps. We're not going to have a McSwain Christmas this year. Our kids want to spend Christmas in their own homes, and so we'll celebrate on Saturday. That's if the weather allows for travel. We're supposed to get a half-inch of ice today and 16-18 inches of snow this week.

Our first Christmas without Grandma Betty and without the gifts she knitted for the grandkids was 2009. The photo is of Mom's great-grandkids modeling their caps and mittens from Christmas a few years earlier.

Susan and Dennis are coming to our house on New Year's Eve afternoon for a while. Remember last year how you wanted us to hire someone to stay with you so the four of us could go out and celebrate? We told you we'd celebrate some other time. Well, we won't be doing a lot of celebrating, but at least we'll spend some time together.

Margo wrote me a nice email the other day. She said she knew it would be difficult for us this Christmas, having you watching from above instead of being beside us. She also said she knew you'd enjoy your first Christmas in heaven. I hadn't thought of that. I hope it's your best Christmas ever, and I hope you know how much we love and miss you, Mom.

Love, Mary

49
One Year

January 12, 2010, marked one year since Mom died. We were at Joe and Nicole's babysitting the grandchildren that evening. After we put the kids to bed, I made a point to leave early so I could be home by myself. At exactly 8:25 p.m., the time of Mom's death, I raised a toast to her.

It was unsettling that I still thought about my mom so often – a full year after her death. Why did I think the grieving process would be over in six months or a year? Isn't that what the books say? If they do, they're wrong. The experts probably say everybody heals differently.

I was still dealing with distributing assets, filing Mom's taxes, and making decisions about the trust. I would cross items off the list with mixed feelings. I desperately wanted to be done with all the trust responsibilities, but, at the same time, taking care of Mom's business made me feel closer to her.

On January 15, I found yet another piece of the puzzle in my search for information about the McSwains. A year had passed since I discovered the McSwain history on Ancestry.com but I still hadn't been able to contact the original author, Linda. Then I joined Facebook. I knew very little about social media, but Steve and I wanted to locate some college friends with whom we'd lost touch, so Laura helped us find them through Facebook.

As I learned more about social media, it occurred to me I might be able to find the author of the McSwain history through Facebook. Even so, I was surprised when I typed her name into the search bar and a post from Linda appeared. I sent a private message asking if she was the same Linda related to my father's mother, Rachel Stewart McSwain. I didn't have to wait long. Her response came the same day:

I am SO excited you found me. Isn't Facebook wonderful? We'll have lots of chats from now on. I contacted Rob McSwain, who is your half-brother, Frank Sr.'s son, in 2004, and we chatted for a while, but then I lost contact with him. My great-aunt told me about your brother Michael coming to Paris, TN, trying to find his roots. I'm sad that no one put him in contact with me. I'm sad that he passed away without me knowing him.

Rachel Stewart McSwain is my great-aunt & her husband Dale McSwain was my great-uncle, so yes — I guess that makes us cousins on down the line.

Linda and I have since exchanged several emails and are Facebook friends, so we've been able to stay in touch. We hope to meet in person someday.

50
Two Sure Things

March 30, 2010

Dear Mom,

It's been a while since I've written. I wish I could say I don't think of you as often anymore, but in fact, I think about you all the time. Everything reminds me of you. There are times when I still can't believe you're gone, and other times when you seem so far away. It's like the reading, "Gone from our Sight," included in hospice materials. A ship disappears from sight, and from our vantage point, the ship gets smaller and smaller; but of course, the ship doesn't change in size at all. It's just our perspective.

Susan and Dennis came here on your birthday, and we went out to eat. We decided we'd always try to get together on your birthday.

Steve did your taxes. You'd be horrified to know that you had to pay a little over $10,000 in federal taxes! I remember a couple of years ago when some of your savings bonds matured, so you cashed them in and had to pay a big IRS bill. You were not happy. We were able to save some on your taxes by strategically cashing the bonds over two years.

We finally figured out how to handle your IRA and arranged for payout every year on your birthday. The first check came as scheduled, so it was proof that we'd done it correctly. It's such a relief to have 95% of your affairs taken care of and to know you'd approve of the way we've handled them. It was a lot of work, but I'm proud of the way we dealt with every last detail. We tried to make sure each of your investments got the best return possible.

Remember how we talked about setting up a scholarship in your name while you were still in the hospital? It was such a great idea, and you loved it too. You enjoyed helping Susan and me set the guidelines for the scholarship. We attended the reception for the first recipient, but she didn't show up, and the Foundation Office neglected to tell us she wouldn't be there. We were very disappointed. We finally got to meet her a few weeks later. We liked her, and I think you would, too. Her dad died unexpectedly in a truck accident, and so she had to drop out of classes last semester. She will still graduate in August.

This weekend is Easter. We're getting together with Susan, Dennis, Jill's family, and all of our kids and grandkids Saturday. I have filled 182 eggs for the Easter egg hunt. The weather is beautiful today, and I was hoping for a nice Easter for a change, but it sounds like it will be cool and rainy on Sunday. We'll miss your deviled eggs and your Jell-O eggs, but Nicole Kathleen has promised to bring them in your memory.

You'll be happy to know that I finally worked up the courage to have a colonoscopy. I had almost convinced myself I had colon cancer, but the results were negative. What a relief!

Love, Mary

51
Mother's Day

May 13, 2010

Dear Mom,

Well, another Mother's Day has come and gone. This one wasn't as hard as the first one without you, but I'm stunned at how often I still think about you… (You're probably tired of my whining.) I wake up most mornings thinking about you. At night, you're usually the last thing on my mind before going to sleep. It's kind of crazy, maybe an obsession. But it's getting better. Now I can think of you without always feeling sad.

We didn't do much celebrating on Mother's Day. None of our kids were around, and we didn't go to Sutherland to be with Steve's family. We went to church, took a nap, mowed the lawn, and then went to our small group meeting in the evening. Mother's Day is overrated.

I remember writing a story for Mother's Day when I worked at *The Daily Reporter*. I interviewed a woman in her 70s and asked her some inane question like: "What do you like best about Mother's Day?" She hesitated and then patiently explained to me that Mother's Day wasn't a happy day for a lot of people like her whose mothers have passed away. I realized then how insensitive I had been.

I found the Mother's Day card I gave you decades ago in your valuable papers box. You saved it all these years! I shopped for the card very carefully and finally found the perfect one. It read: "So much of the person I am is because of the mother you are. Thanks, Mom."

You seemed very touched when you read those words. Mom, that is so true, even though you may not have known what a positive influence you had in my life. I learned to be independent, open-minded, caring, and self-reliant from you. Thank you for those gifts.

I've been thinking about how you changed over the years as a mother. I have to say you could be difficult when we were younger. But as we matured and you grew older, you became a different kind of mother. You were more patient, more loving, less controlling, and you truly seemed to enjoy being with us and our children.

I read an essay in the AARP magazine, written by Katherine Nouri Hughes, which included this take on changing as we age:

> ...When we're young we have the advantage of thinking we're going to live forever. When we're older we have the advantage of knowing we won't. We change in a lot of ways over the seasons of our lives. But I now believe that it's when we're older that we have what it takes to willfully change ourselves...

Not all older people change for the better. Some get crankier and harder to live with as they age. A friend told me recently she envied our "close relationship." Her mother had gotten more difficult over the years and, no matter how hard my friend tries, her mom remains almost impossible to please. I told her you and I had our ups and downs, especially when we were both younger. You made the effort to change. I hope it's true of me, too. I wasn't the perfect mother, and there are days when our kids were growing up that I wish I could do over. But I see how my children have matured into responsible caring adults who are good parents to their children. I hope it's because of, and not in spite of, the way they were parented. Maybe it's some of both.

Susan's birthday was two weeks ago, her second without you. Last year was hard for her. You didn't call her to sing "Happy Birthday" bright and early in the morning like you always did when you were here. So, this year, Steve and I called her and sang. It wasn't quite the same, but she appreciated the effort.

Jill and I hosted a surprise retirement and 60th birthday party for Susan at the Lake View Shelter. (Can you believe your oldest daughter is 60?) She was so surprised! About 60 friends, co-workers, and family members came. Nicole Kathleen made a beautiful cake, and Laura took pictures. You would have enjoyed it.

One of your neighbors, Mae, died last week. You know how you always helped her when she had low blood sugar or insulin shock? And when you put drops in her eyes several times a day after her cataract surgery? She was diagnosed with pancreatic cancer around the time you died and had been in a lot of pain at the end. They moved her to a nursing home even though she didn't want to leave Golfview.

Mae and her daughter talked with medical staff, and Mae told them she didn't want any more treatment, including her insulin. I'm hoping she went into a coma and died more peacefully than if she had waited for cancer to cause her death. She was such a nice person. One morning when you were so sick and at home, Susan and I heard a light tap on your condo door. When we opened it, there was Mae with a plate of warm muffins and a "thinking of you" note, even though she had just received a terminal diagnosis herself.

I had a conference in Wisconsin Dells last week. I decided to attend mostly because of the location, and Steve went with me. It was a sentimental journey – traveling along the Kickapoo River, going through La Crosse where we spent our wedding night, and seeing the area again.

Wisconsin Dells has changed so much. I remember the "Tommy Bartlett Show" being out in the country, and now the city is built up all around it. It's mile after mile of water park resorts. I liked it better the way it was when you took us there as kids, or even when we took our kids there almost 30 years ago. I think now what a big deal it was that you would take us to Wisconsin Dells for a family vacation. I'm sure money was tight, and taking three little kids on a car trip had to have been challenging.

I am just about done with my job as successor trustee. I wrote the last checks to your heirs yesterday. We've paid the trust's income taxes for 2009, and the only expense left to pay is $1,000 this year and $1,000 next year for your nursing scholarship. It's kind of sad, but I will be happy to finally close out your accounts.

Last week, Susan and I, along with Joe and two other Iowa Lakes nursing instructors, picked the second Elizabeth McSwain Nursing Scholarship recipient. I am sure you would think she is an excellent choice. Her name is Joan and is a few years younger than I am, has raised three sons, and her instructors say she'll be a great nurse. She told us she felt a real connection to you. Besides both of you being nurses, she also loves to travel. She wrote this note:

To the Donors of the Elizabeth McSwain Scholarships,

Thank you for choosing me as the recipient of this award. When I saw the letter in my email last night, I was overwhelmed. This will help me so much. I will now be able to focus on my studies without worrying about the mounting debt. I am very proud to read about Elizabeth, knowing what an awesome nurse she was. I hope to carry that spirit into my nursing career.

Joan

Joan wrote another note before her graduation:

   ...*I am in my final semester of nursing school. It has been a challenging year but the goal is in sight. I keep Elizabeth's picture by my desk. It encourages me daily to strive toward the goal. Thank you so much.*

Joan

   I'm sure you'd agree, Mom, Joan is a great choice for the scholarship. Whenever I see her around town, she gives me a hug!

Love, Mary

52
More Goodbyes

August 30, 2010

Dear Mom,

Two people you cared about died this month – your nephew, Gene, and your friend, Bonnie. They died just a few hours apart and both funerals were on the same day. We had to choose which one to attend. It was a difficult choice, but we went to Gene's. I felt like this might be the last time we would get back to Readstown. Gene was our last blood relative living in the area.

Gene's funeral was at the Readstown Advancement Building, and it was packed. Marilyn *(Gene's wife)* was happy to see us, and it was nice for us to see cousins Annette and Nancy.

Bonnie's funeral was in Marcus, and Margo *(my friend and Bonnie's daughter)* said it went well. Her last conversation with Bonnie was on a Sunday afternoon. Margo had gone to the hospice place directly from our camping weekend, and although Bonnie was very weak, she was able to communicate with Margo and her brother. Margo said they had a nice conversation. Bonnie died the next morning at about 6:30 a.m.

Bonnie wrote a letter to you on January 11, 2009 and mailed it on January 12, the day you died. Since you never got to read it, here it is:

Dear Betty,

I just want you to know how much I have appreciated your friendship all these years. I have enjoyed your company on all of the trips we took and the golf we played – even though I was not a good player!!

...Betty, I hope you are getting along without pain, and I know you are glad to be in your own place. You know without my saying how very sorry I am of what you are going through. You have my many prayers and I know God is with you. Take care.

Much love and prayers,
Bonnie

Margo and I are picturing our moms running hand in hand through fields of flowers in heaven.

We are all doing pretty well. When you were sick, you asked us several times if we were going to be okay. We assured you we would be, but it's been harder than I expected, and it's taken much longer than I thought it would. If nothing else, I've learned to be more empathetic when people lose their parents. I've also come to realize how much notes of sympathy mean to someone who's grieving.

I have so enjoyed exchanging emails with Cynthia McSwain, the cousin I never knew I had. She sounds so interesting and warm. We're going to try to get together soon. I wish you could have shared this experience with me. If only I had started looking for the McSwains a few months earlier.

Love, Mary

53
Rob McSwain

September 2010, brought another surprise in my quest to find out more about my dad's family. On September 1, completely out of the blue, the name "Rob McSwain" popped up in my email inbox.

From: Rob McSwain
Subject: Arch Dale McSwain Jr
To: Mary Steele
Date: Wednesday, September 1, 2010

Mary,

I believe you spoke to my cousin, Debbie. I am Rob McSwain, Arch Dale's grandson. I never met him and know very little about him. I would be interested to hear what you found out!

I found your email on a genealogy site after Debbie mentioned that she had spoken to you. Feel free to reply to this email or look for me on Facebook.

Thanks,
Rob McSwain

Rob was one of two sons born to my half-brother, Frank. Frank's mother was my dad's first wife. Their marriage lasted only a couple of years.

I read Rob's email several times before responding.

From: Mary Steele
Sent: Wednesday, September 01, 2010
To: Rob McSwain
Subject: Re: Arch Dale McSwain Jr

Wow! It's not often the name "McSwain" pops up on my email account. What a nice surprise!

My mom, Elizabeth (Betty) McSwain, was Arch Dale Jr.'s second wife. Mom died last year, which is what motivated me to find out more about my dad's family. Like you, I also knew very little about him. He and my mom separated when I was about 4 years old, and it made her sad to talk about our dad, so we didn't ask her much about him. I don't think she ever met his parents, but she may have met his brother, Warren.

I had done some Internet searches several years ago but came up with nothing until just last year when I found Debbie's post on a genealogy web site. I will be forever grateful to her for paving the way for me to find out about my dad and his family.

My mom and dad were married only briefly, but long enough to have three children: my sister, Susan, was born in 1950; I was born in 1951; and my brother, Michael, was born in 1953. My brother died in 2001, and his daughter, Leslie, is the only one of us left whose last name is McSwain. My sister and I both use our married names.

In about 1977, my brother decided to try to find out more about our dad's family, so he went to Tennessee to visit his half-brother, your dad. I have pictures of them together. Your dad gave Mike some serving pieces of the McSwain silverware and a bottle from the McSwain Pharmacy, which I now have.

Through Debbie, I was able to locate Warren's daughter, Cynthia McSwain, who lives in San Antonio, TX. I hope to meet her soon.

It would be great to meet you sometime as well. My husband,

Steve, and I live in northwest Iowa and have enjoyed vacationing in Michigan. What city do you live in? Do you have a family? You have a brother, Frank Jr, right? I am also on Facebook.

Enough for now, but I hope we can continue this conversation. It's a little like getting part of my childhood back if that makes any sense.

My brother, Mike, visiting Rob's dad, Frank, in about 1977.

Rob responded later that day:

From: Rob McSwain
Subject: RE: Arch Dale McSwain Jr
To: Mary Steele
Date: Wednesday, September 1, 2010

Thanks for your reply!

I vaguely remember your brother meeting up with my Dad. He never spoke much of his father. I know he left them when he was young. I am sure it was a sore spot for him.

I'm sure it was tough on your mother and my grandmother back then. Being a single mother in the '50s is a lot different than it is now. My mother's father did the same thing, so it seems like I have two *huge gaping holes in my history.*

    Despite his penchant for running off, I am very interested in him and the McSwain side of the family. After talking to Debbie, I did some searching and probably found some of the information that you located. Did you see his yearbook picture on the EW Grove High School website? It is listed as just Dale McSwain, but it has to be him.

    I live in Alpena. It is in Northeast Michigan. I have a daughter, Taylor, and a brother Frankie, who lives in Pickwick, TN.

    I will look for you on Facebook. It would be awesome to meet up! Thanks again for your email. If you had any pictures that could be scanned and emailed, I would love to see them.

Rob

Rob and I exchanged some family pictures and a few messages. He's a Facebook friend, so I keep up with his posts.

Rob and Kristal McSwain

After our first email exchange, Rob and his wife, Kristal, moved back to Tennessee. When Steve and I were getting ready to drive to an out-of-state wedding in 2018, it occurred to me we'd be spending our first night on the road in the town where Rob and Kristal lived. I asked Rob if he'd like to get together, and he said he would.

Rob and Kristal met us at a restaurant where we thoroughly enjoyed getting to know them. When it got late, Rob asked if we'd like to meet him for breakfast to continue our conversation, and so we did. I think Rob and I felt like we'd known each other for a long time. The main thing we had in common was that we were both searching for information about my absent dad and his absent grandfather.

54
We Finally Meet

Jan. 4, 2011

Dear Mom,

A new year. This is the year I'll turn 60. I'm trying to remember when you were 60. That would have been in 1984. Our kids would have been just 11, 9, and 7.

Steve and I wanted to go someplace warm over the holiday break, so we went to Corpus Christi and South Padre Island, Texas for a couple of weeks after Christmas. I hadn't heard from Cynthia McSwain – my cousin, your niece – for several months, so I decided not to contact her to say we'd be coming right through San Antonio.

But halfway there, I changed my mind. I emailed Cynthia from our hotel in Ardmore, Oklahoma, to see if she might want to meet for lunch. She responded right away and said they were at their vacation home in Arizona. She sounded disappointed that we weren't going to get a chance to meet. Cynthia apologized for not writing. She said she was working on a long letter to me that would explain things. She shared a lot of family history in her letter, some of it quite personal. She may have thought the information might adversely affect our relationship, but I was honored she trusted me enough to share her family's story with me.

We've been emailing back and forth frequently since she wrote the letter. We also exchanged family pictures. The photos she sent of my dad and her dad as little boys are priceless. Cynthia says Mike looks very much like her late brother, Warren.

I wish we had known about Cynthia before you died. I think you would have enjoyed getting to know each other. Although I haven't met her in person yet, I feel like I know her already.

Cynthia's father, Warren, at left, his mother, Rachel, and my dad, Mac (Arch Dale Jr.). The photo was taken around 1930.

Over Christmas, Joe and Nicole and family visited Nicole's parents near Phoenix. They took a day and went to South Mountain to find the memorial spot. They exchanged text messages and phone calls with us back in Iowa while looking for the exact location. They finally found it, confirmed by sending a picture to our phone. We were so pleased that they had made the effort. Steve and I will go back there sometime, too. You and Mike won't be forgotten.

Love, Mary

In January 2012, while on the way to visit friends in Arizona, we made arrangements to visit Cynthia and Orion. I was nervous but excited, and I'm guessing she felt the same way. Within a few minutes after arriving at their home, I felt like we were old friends. I gave her pictures of all her "new" cousins and she was delighted. She went from having only one blood relative (her brother, John) to having two first-cousins (Susan and me), five second-cousins (Susan's daughter, Mike's daughter, and my children), and fourteen third-cousins (our grandchildren).

After we returned to Iowa, I received a card from Cynthia with the following message, which sums up exactly how I felt, too:

Meeting you last week was one of the most meaningful events of my life. What an exceptional thing! I remain utterly amazed at the magic of my new, astonishing family. You've given me quite a gift. The pictures have been shown to everyone I know here. I just cannot thank you enough for finding me.

There is a litany of gratitudes I have actually. Not the least of which is Steve. He is just wonderful, and I (and Orion) look forward to getting to know him better. Please thank him for being so great during our visit — lots of time for you and me plus full of interesting talk for Orion (who had a very good time). Thank you also for the gifts. I'm afraid the candy is gone, and I was very selfish about it. But the rest of the gifts remain and mean so much to me. How gracious, generous, and thoughtful you are.

Which brings me to you, for which I am most grateful. You've changed my life in the richest, fullest sense.

Much love, Cynthia

Since our first visit, Cynthia has been to our home in

Iowa. She met all of our children and grandchildren in a whirlwind tour of Iowa while she was here. Steve and I went to Arizona a second time to visit Cynthia and Orion, and we met her brother, John McSwain, and his wife, Linda. We continue to exchange emails and texts. I realize now we probably never would have met Cynthia and Orion had it not been for Mom's death – and Jack's family tree assignment – which prompted my search for the McSwains.

My first cousin Cynthia McSwain and me.

55
Sharing Mom's Story

November 4, 2011

Dear Mom,

Whoa! Can it be that I haven't written to you in nine months? Or did I lose part of the computer file with my letters to you? I'm not sure. Maybe I've substituted writing to you with writing your story. I now have more than 60 pages in a very rough form for the "book." Sometimes I think it has potential, and other times I wonder why I'm doing it.

But then I remind myself that my main goal isn't to write a bestselling memoir or even get it published. I'm writing it for my kids and grandkids so they'll remember you – and me, too, I guess. As with the letters I've written to you, writing the book has been good for me. I'm surprised by how much I've enjoyed the research and writing.

This is the time of year when the annual Nursing Scholarship Donor Reception is held at Iowa Lakes Community College. I was asked to be the speaker. Steve and Joe were there to represent our family, as well as other donors, recipients, and college administrators.

Here's an edited version of what I said about the Elizabeth McSwain Nursing Scholarship:

Elizabeth Anna Rosson McSwain was a registered nurse, an avid golfer, a world traveler, a nature lover, and a capable and independent woman. She was also my mother. She raised three children alone from the time we were 2, 4, and 5 years old.

After we went off to college, my mom was free to pursue her lifelong dream of seeing the world. She applied for a nursing position and was hired to work at the King Faisal Specialist Hospital in Riyadh, Saudi Arabia. For every 11 months she worked, she earned one month off to travel. She took full advantage of the opportunity to see the world, traveling throughout the Middle East, Europe, Africa, and points beyond, usually with coworkers, but sometimes by herself.
After retiring, Mom moved to Spencer to be closer to her children and grandchildren. She worked for several years as a part-time proctor at the Spencer campus of Iowa Lakes Community College. She led a healthy, active life...

It was a shock to all of us when Mom was diagnosed with endometrial cancer in December 2008. There was nothing the doctors could do for her. She died at home just a month and a day after her diagnosis, lovingly cared for by her two daughters. Although the time was too short, we were so thankful to have those few weeks to reminisce, to ask her questions about her life, and to say our goodbyes ...

I shared how much your nursing degree meant to you, Mom. I told them that you loved being a nurse, that your patients and co-workers said you were very good at your job. I told them about the scholarship idea, that you helped set the guidelines. And I talked about how you had experienced caregiving from both sides – as a nurse and as a patient. I closed with this:

Being terminally ill gave Mom a new perspective on the difference that a caring, compassionate, and skilled nurse could make during such an impossibly difficult time. She would be so pleased to see that she had a small part in helping others to pursue a career in nursing.

I think other donors can relate when I say the scholarship has meant as much to our family as to the recipients.

     What better way to honor our mother and preserve her memory than to help students reach their goal of becoming nurses.

I hope you liked it, Mom.

Love, Mary

56
I'm Okay

January 12, 2020

Dear Mom,

We are in Gulf Shores, Alabama, in a condo on the beach with a beautiful view of the gulf and white sand. I am listening to the roar of the ocean and watching the gulls fly by as I type. It's early afternoon and the sun is just breaking through the fog. You would love it here!

Today is Sunday. Steve and I went to church at Florabama, which gets its name from its location on the Florida-Alabama state line. Florabama is a large sprawling roadhouse with two restaurants, several bars, a dance hall, a souvenir store, and a meeting place for a church. Rustic doesn't quite describe the building. Dilapidated? Ramshackle? Rickety? No, those words might be too strong. Let's just say that an architect was probably not involved in designing it, and the lumber to build it has rarely seen paint.

I thought of you throughout the service. You always preferred a non-traditional service, and the Florabama worship service is definitely non-traditional. The part of the roadhouse that's used for the church is a permanent tent with a circus-like canvas top and canvas walls that can be rolled up in nice weather and rolled down when it's cold or rainy. The floors are made of thick unfinished boards installed at an angle. Instead of pews, there are white plastic folding chairs. Everyone picks up their chairs after the service and moves them against the wall because the worship area doubles as the dance hall and Bingo room.

The church provides free coffee, but I noticed several churchgoers holding Bloody Marys they had purchased as they walked by the bars on the way into worship. That may have made us cringe just a little, growing up in a conservative church, but this is one church where you leave judgments at the door.

The praise band was very good. I'm guessing they used to play in dance halls and bars – maybe they still do. My favorite of the songs we sang was "Amazing Grace," which I know is one of your favorites, too. However, this version of "Amazing Grace" was set to the tune of "The House of the Rising Sun." It's hard not to smile when the praise band plays that one.

Today was a nice day, so the canvas side walls were rolled up. Birds flew in one opening and out another throughout the service, frequently swooping directly over our heads. You would have especially appreciated that.

The church's motto is "It's okay not to be okay." (Our counselor friend, Gary, adds a caveat to the motto: "But it's not okay to stay that way.") The church is made up of a diverse group of people of all ages. Most wear jeans and casual shirts, often t-shirts or sweatshirts with their favorite sports team logos or places where they've vacationed.

But many were dressed up as if they were going to a traditional service in a traditional church building with a steeple, stained glass windows, and maybe a pipe organ. I saw an older woman in a real fur vest who was with a man in an expensive-looking black suit with a nicely pressed white dress shirt and gold cuff links. Homeless people sometimes attend the services, usually standing just outside the open side walls with their possessions in backpacks or paper bags. The church has a food pantry and regular meetings for people in recovery. It's the kind of church, I think, Jesus meant for the church to be. A church where everyone feels welcome.

The sermon was about "Discerning Truth." One of the scripture verses was Proverbs 3:5, "Trust in the Lord with all of your heart and lean not upon your own understanding. In all your ways acknowledge Him and He shall direct your paths."

It was 11 years ago today that you died. I've done a lot of leaning on God since then, and I've learned to trust Him more. Working through my grief has not been easy and has taken much longer than I anticipated. Before you died, I truly believed I'd be fine. I had a supportive husband, three children, their spouses, and 10 grandchildren to fill the void.

It's been slow, but I want you to know I have made significant progress towards healing in the last 11 years. When I think of you now, instead of remembering you when you were sick and frail, I think of the many happy times we had together as a family: holiday and birthday celebrations, picnics, biking vacations, Broadway musicals, grandkids' music and sports events. Writing these letters and this memoir has helped me heal, along with the love and kindness of friends and family.

I've decided to use proceeds from the book (if there are any) to start a scholarship fund. I envision it being awarded to students wishing to pursue a career in nursing. I know you'd be happy about that. I can feel you smiling.

The Bible says that everything works together for good for those who love God. As difficult as it was to see you so sick and frail, I am grateful for the way your illness brought the three of us closer together. The last thirty-two days we spent with you was a very special time. Susan and I went from seeing each other once every couple of months to spending every day together with you. We had so many meaningful conversations. You seemed peaceful and content as long as we were together.

After you died, Susan and I kept in touch through email and phone calls almost every day. Despite our grief, and probably because of it, we are closer than we've ever been before. There was also the unexpected bonus of finding Cynthia and Rob and other relatives I never knew I had. I guess it's like you told us during bad storms, "Rain makes the flowers grow."

I need to share a recent experience that was meaningful for me. I found my dad's grave yesterday. I was looking through letters Mike had written 30 years ago, and I found one in which he wrote about trying to locate our father's gravesite. After some research, he found out Mac was buried in Ft. Walton Beach, Florida, where he worked at the hospital as a lab tech. When he died in 1962, no one knew how to contact his family, so a group of hospital employees chipped in and bought a plot for his burial.

For 32 years, there was no marker at our dad's grave. It remained unmarked until Mike visited it in 1996. He applied to the Veterans Administration for a marker, and they supplied one. I don't think Mike ever got to see the marker, but hopefully the VA or the cemetery sent him a picture.

Ft. Walton Beach is just two hours from Gulf Shores, so Steve and I decided to go there and look for the gravesite. Mike said in the letter, "If you ever visit the Beal Cemetery in Ft. Walton, the caretaker can tell you where the grave is. As I remember, it is on the west entrance, about seven or eight rows up, not far from the caretaker's building."

When we got to the cemetery, we decided not to ask the caretaker for help finding the grave, even though it was a very large cemetery. I wanted us to find it for ourselves, based on Mike's letter. Steve and I decided we'd each take a row and look for the VA plaque marking Arch Dale McSwain's gravesite. We found it within a few minutes.

The marker looks nice, but the gravesite was a little plain. We went to a local kite-and-flag store, bought a pretty stars-and-stripes garden flag, and returned to the cemetery to put it next to the marker. It looks so nice! We also bought an identical one for outside the front entrance of our house. It is a reminder of him.

My dad's gravesite.

Once we'd planted the garden flag and took some pictures, Steve went to the car. I stayed a few minutes longer so I could talk to my dad. I told him about you and our family – his children, his grandchildren, and his great-grandchildren. I told him I loved him.

It went through my mind, while standing near the grave, that this was the closest I'd been to my father in more than 60 years. It was an emotional, but satisfying, experience.

In reading through Mike's letters and learning that he, too, had a desire to find our dad, I felt closer to my brother than I ever remembered us being. He ends his last letter to me by saying, "Be good, and even though we never say it, you know that I love you, along with Susan and Mom. Thanks again for being there."

There's another discovery I want to share with you,

Mom. I was on Facebook last night and I noticed a woman had commented on one of my posts, but I didn't recognize her as a Facebook friend. I clicked on her picture and then her "About" information, and I realized it was Debbie Olson's sister Laurie!

We have exchanged several messages, and I will send Facebook friend requests to Debbie's other sisters, Mary and Karen. After all these years of no communication with the Olson family, I didn't expect to hear from them again. Their parents have both passed away. I hope to visit Laurie, Mary, and Karen sometime in Wisconsin.

I wish I could tell you I have found your first-born child, the baby you gave up for adoption. I haven't. We will keep trying. *Inshallah*, perhaps he will read this memoir and recognize his biological mother's name. I know it's an incredible longshot, but stranger things have happened during this journey.

You asked Susan and me 11 years ago, "Will you be okay?"

I can finally say, "I'm okay." When I think of you now, I smile. I can talk about you without tearing up.

So many times while writing the memoir, I started sentences with "If only," or "I wish" we had done something differently. I think it's a sign of healing when I can put the regrets behind me and think only of the happy times. I even got out and displayed the red Ho-Ho-Ho fleece blanket this past Christmas!

Mom, I think you'll understand when I tell you this is the last letter I'll write to you. It's time to let you go. I don't want you to worry about me anymore. (Is worrying even allowed in heaven?)

I've read that one of the biggest fears people have about dying is the fear of being forgotten. You'll be in my thoughts often and always in my heart. And you won't be forgotten by your grandchildren or great-grandchildren, because they'll have these words to get to know you better and to remember you.

You gave us the gift of being closer as a family. This memoir is my gift to you.

I love you, Mom.
Mary

Gone from My Sight

I am standing upon the seashore. A ship, at my side, spreads her white sails to the morning breeze and starts for the blue ocean. She is an object of beauty and strength.

I stand and watch her until, at length, she hangs like a speck of a white cloud just where the sea and sky come to mingle with each other.

Then someone at my side says: "There, she is gone!"

Gone where? Gone from my sight. That is all.

She is just as large in mast and hull and spar as she was when she left my side, and she is just as able to bear the load of living freight to her destined port.

Her diminished size is in me, not in her. And just at the moment when someone at my side says "There, she is gone," there are other eyes watching her coming, and other voices ready to take up the glad shout, "Here she comes!"

And that is dying.

- Henry Van Dyke

Watercolor by Elizabeth McSwain

In Appreciation

I am grateful to my manuscript readers who slogged through various drafts and provided helpful feedback and constant encouragement: Cynthia McSwain, Mary Frank, Jane Nolan Goeken, Lora Zeutenhorst, Tom and Margo Gates, Nancy Schoville, John and Millie Mandernach, Gretchen Dennis, and Anna Eckert.

I owe a debt of gratitude to my friend, classmate, and genealogy enthusiast, Leanne Granger Newman, who read two drafts of the manuscript, spent many hours researching the McSwains and the Rossons, and encouraged me with every text she sent.

Thanks also to Debbie Killebrew Mallard and Linda Stewart Reed who posted the McSwain history on Ancestry.com. That post was my first clue in discovering information about my father that I thought was forever lost. I also appreciate the help of Janice Rogers, the supervisor at Beal Memorial Cemetery in Fort Walton Beach, Florida, who graciously looked through cemetery records to answer questions about my father's gravesite.

A special thank you to Sarah Smith who let us photograph her daughter, sweet Lila, for the cover of this memoir. From the day I decided to write this book, I had a vision stored away in my mind of a little red-haired girl on the cover. The little girl could be my mom, my sister, my daughter, or me.

Thanks to Laura Steele Eckert who took the cover photograph. It can't be easy getting a toddler to stand still for a picture, much less follow commands like: look down, look serious, smell the flower — all as Lila joyfully plucked off each petal one by one!

I can't say enough about Spencer Hospital and Hospice staff. They provided quality care, information, and advice with compassion and kindness when we needed it most.

One of the unexpected pleasures of working on this book is that I've connected with people I hadn't seen since high school. Laurie Olson, my best friend Debbie Olson's younger sister, reached out to me through Facebook just as I was finishing the book. Laurie provided details about Debbie I didn't know, and she sent photos of Debbie to use in this memoir. I've since become Facebook friends with her sisters, Mary and Karen.

I am blessed that our children enthusiastically agreed to be part of this memoir process. Joe and Nicole Kathleen Steele, Aaron and Nicole Maria Steele, and Laura and David Eckert read several versions of the manuscript and offered great advice. They also encouraged me to write the book for a larger audience than just my family and close friends, which was my original intent. Laura also did all the formatting, edited all the photos, and took my author headshot, cover photo, and other pictures included in the book.

Thanks to our grandchildren who are always a source of inspiration and delight and have brought so much joy to our lives: Jack, Timothy, Allison, Anna, Sam, Charlie, Benjamin, Trevor, Rowan, and Caleb.

I am especially grateful to my husband, Steve, who was beside me throughout this 11-year journey. He provided emotional support, helped with research, offered constant encouragement, and never doubted my ability to get it done. He has been my husband, partner, and friend for 49 years.

We've only just begun, Steve!

To contact the author, email
marysteele444@gmail.com.

Reference for Readers

The Rossons

Albert & Ellyn Rosson: My mother's parents, my grandparents.

Their children: Alice, Raymond, and Elizabeth (Betty), my mother (1924-2009).

Nancy and Annette Glass: My first cousins, two of my Aunt Alice's and Uncle Earl's daughters.

The McSwains

Arch Dale McSwain Sr. & Rachel Stewart McSwain: My father's parents, my grandparents.

Arch Dale McSwain Jr. (Mac): My dad (1921-1962). Married Betty Rosson (1924-2009), my mom, in 1949.

Their children: Susan Dale McSwain Garvin, Mary Ellen McSwain Steele, Michael Rosson McSwain (1953-2001).

Warren Sr. & June Simmons McSwain: My dad's younger brother and his wife, my uncle and aunt.

Their children: My first cousins, Warren Jr., (also called Mac, died in 1995), Cynthia, and John McSwain.

Rob McSwain: My half-nephew, grandson of my dad and his first wife, Marian. Mac and Marian had a son, Frank. He had two sons, Frankie and Rob. Rob is married to Kristal.

The Steeles

Steven Steele: My husband, married in 1971.

Our children: Joseph (Nicole K.) Steele, Aaron (Nicole M.) Steele & Laura Steele (David) Eckert.

Our grandchildren: Timothy, Allison, Charlie, and Trevor Steele; Jack, Sam, and Rowan Steele; Anna, Benjamin, and Caleb Eckert.

Other People Mentioned Frequently

Debbie Olson: My best friend from first grade through our weddings.

Greg Guinn: My brother Mike's best friend and former partner.

Leanne Granger Newman: Friend, classmate, and historian/genealogy enthusiast.

Linda and Debbie: Their posts on Ancestry.com and many follow-up emails helped me uncover important information about my dad's family.

McSwain Family of Henry County, Tennessee
(This is the full McSwain family history referenced in Chapter 37.)

The McSwain family was among the early settlers of this country, having left Scotland for America, arriving in Pennsylvania in 1731. The family moved to Virginia and then North Carolina in 1765.

...In December 1868, Isaac Arnold McSwain (my great-grandfather), a farmer and a doctor, married Margaret Ann Dale, Dr. Isaac A. and Margaret had 11 children...The youngest was Arch Dale (my grandfather), born in 1893.

Arch "Dale," a graduate of E.W. Grove High School, was a member of the First Methodist Church and the local Masonic order. He worked as a clerk for the L & N Railroad, was later in insurance, and also a photographer. On April 20, 1919, he married Rachel Stewart, daughter of James Warren Stewart and Nora Irene Brizendine Stewart.

The couple had two sons, Arch "Dale, Jr." (my dad, nicknamed "Mac") and Warren. Dale Sr. died of heart disease at the age of 42 on Jan. 15, 1936. Rachel was active in church work, with a quiet and gentle manner but was also in ill health, and, after her husband's death, she and the two boys moved to Puryear to live with her widowed mother Nora who had remarried to Coil Paschall.

In 1937, Dale Jr. went to live with his uncle, Dr. George McSwain. Warren continued to live with his mother until entering Lambuth College. He married June Simmons and continued his education at the SMU graduate school in Dallas. Rachel, who was bedridden with heart disease and tuberculosis, was moved to Upland Sanitarium in Pleasant Hill, TN, where she died November 18, 1954. Dale Sr. and Rachel are buried in Maplewood Cemetery.

Dale Jr. married Marian Killebrew Ross and had one son, Frank Dale (1946). Dale Jr. later moved to Florida, remarried, and had a son, Michael. Frank Dale McSwain was a postal carrier in Paris, Tennessee. He married Susan Irene Richardson and had 2 sons, William (called "Frankie") and

Robert (called "Rob"). Frank died in 1998 and is buried in Hillcrest Cemetery.

Warren became a Methodist minister and later an executive with Texas Wired Sound. He and June lived in Texas where they had three children, Cynthia, Warren Jr., and John. Cynthia is married and lives in Texas. John, a bachelor, lives in Virginia, and Warren Jr. nicknamed "Mac" died of Wilson's disease in 1985.

Made in the USA
Monee, IL
12 October 2022

15718941R00148